100

MORNINGS
&EVENINGS

IN HIS PRESENCE

Destiny Image Books by Bill Johnson

Resting Place

The Way of Life

The Power of Communion (with Beni)

God Is Good

Friendship with God

Hosting the Presence

Hosting the Presence Every Day

When Heaven Invades Earth

The Supernatural Power of the Transformed Mind

Strengthen Yourself in the Lord

Releasing the Spirit of Prophecy

Dreaming with God

Here Comes Heaven

Release the Power of Jesus

The Supernatural Ways of Royalty

Spiritual Java

A Life of Miracles

Center of the Universe

Dream Journal

Destiny Image Books by Beni Johnson

The Power of Communion

40 Days to Wholeness: Body, Soul, and Spirit:

A Healthy and Free Devotional

Healthy and Free

The Happy Intercessor

The Joy of Intercession: A 40 Day Encounter (Happy Intercessor Devotional)

Walking in the Supernatural (with Bill Johnson)

100
MORNINGS
&EVENINGS
IN HIS PRESENCE

*a guided journal for
daily encounters with God*

BILL & BENI
JOHNSON

DESTINY IMAGE® PUBLISHERS, INC.
PO Box 310, Shippensburg, PA 17257-0310
"Promoting Inspired Lives"

This book and all other Destiny Image and Destiny Image Fiction books are available at Christian bookstores and distributors worldwide.

For more information on foreign distributors, call 717-532-3040.

Or reach us on the Internet: www.destinyimage.com

ISBN 13 TP: 978-0-7684-6368-2

For Worldwide Distribution, Printed in the USA

1 2 3 4 5 6 / 25 24 23 22

Contents

Introduction

100 Mornings and Evenings in His Presence—A Guided Journal for Daily Encounters With God complements our book *Mornings and Evenings in His Presence.* This guided journal is designed to provoke exciting new thoughts, imaginative ideas, and spiritual stirrings to bring you closer to your heavenly Father—and to your authentic self as well. Rather than a canned workbook-type journal with elementary fill-in-the-blanks or multiple-choice exercises, the prompts in this guided journal encourage you into a free-flowing, creative environment—open to whatever the Lord brings to the surface of your spirit, mind, and soul.

The content of each Morning page is geared to energize your day in the best way possible—first with a Scripture from the Bible; then a paragraph or two of insightful reflections on the passage; followed by journaling prompts to stir up responses that plant seeds of positivity, which will simmer and stew during the day, creating a whole new perspective on God's Word and how it affects your life for the better.

The Evening pages provide a wind-down time of relaxation via a Scripture verse or passage, an excerpt from the *Mornings and Evenings in His Presence* book, and then prompts to generate responses that bring you to a peaceful place of rest—physically and spiritually—as you put yourself to bed.

We pray that you will enjoy this guided journal as it helps you explore your role in entering and maintaining a place in His Presence day after day and night after night.

You make known to
me the path of life;
in your presence there
is fullness of joy;
at your right hand are
pleasures forevermore.

Psalm 16:11

Fresh Treasures

However, as it is written: "What no eye has seen, what no ear has heard, and what no human mind has conceived"—the things God has prepared for those who love him...The Spirit searches all things, even the deep things of God.

(1 Corinthians 2:9-10 NIV)

The Holy Spirit searches for what has never been heard or seen by human ears or eyes. He is the greatest Search Engine in the universe, searching the greatest reservoir of information imaginable—the heart of the Father. For infinity past, God has been thinking about us—about you—and the Holy Spirit searches that voluminous archive to bring incredibly fresh treasures to you at precisely the right moment—if you're listening.

When I think about the greatness of God, I'm overwhelmed with...

_____

_____

_____

_____

I have recently been having fresh thoughts about...

_____

_____

_____

_____

Day 1

He Knows You

...God now unveils these profound realities to us by the Spirit. Yes, he has revealed to us his inmost heart and deepest mysteries through the Holy Spirit, who constantly explores all things.

(1 Corinthians 2:9-10 TPT)

God has been living in the experience of knowing you long before you were ever born. His thoughts of you are constant and enduring. What He says will always be better than anything you could have thought up yourself. These new ideas may be impossible for you to accomplish in your own strength—so draw close to Him.

Thinking about how "God has been living in the experience of knowing" me is absolutely the most...

_____

_____

_____

_____

In my own strength, I can hardly manage _____;
but with God's power in my life I can handle...

_____

_____

_____

_____

Day 2

Holy Spirit Power

But you shall receive power when the Holy Spirit has come upon you;
and you shall be witnesses to Me in Jerusalem, and in all
Judea and Samaria, and to the end of the earth.

(Acts 1:8 NKJV)

The Holy Spirit lives in born-again believers. The amazing promise that accompanies this reality is that He will never leave us. What a promise. What a comfort. The Holy Spirit rests upon a person because He has been given an honorable welcome. The Holy Spirit is the single greatest reference point for direction and power in every aspect of life. You've been chosen to carry the Presence of God. Amazing!

The responsibility of knowing the Holy Spirit dwells in me can be...

_____

_____

_____

_____

With the power that comes with the Holy Spirit, I am emboldened enough to...

_____

_____

_____

_____

EVENING

A Powerful Witness

After his baptism, as Jesus came up out of the water, the heavens were opened and he saw the Spirit of God descending like a dove and settling on him.

(Matthew 3:16 NLT)

...And you will be my witnesses, telling people about me everywhere—in Jerusalem, throughout Judea, in Samaria, and to the ends of the earth.

(Acts 1:8 NLT)

When I ask people how they would go about their day if an actual dove landed on their shoulder, the most common answer is, "Carefully." A good answer, but not enough. Every step must be with the dove in mind—which is the key for the Spirit to remain.

Picturing the Dove sitting on my shoulder gives me the courage to...

_____

_____

Tomorrow I will still make a conscious effort to take every step "carefully" and...

_____

_____

_____

_____

Day 3

Walking by Faith

*For we walk by faith, not by sight [living our lives in a manner
consistent with our confident belief in God's promises].*

(2 Corinthians 5:7 AMP)

Faith is the mirror of the heart reflecting the realities of an unseen world—
the actual substance of God's Kingdom. Through faith we can pull the reality
of His world into this one. God's Word contrasts the faith life with the lim-
itations of natural sight. Faith provides eyes for the heart, and Jesus expects
people to see from the heart. The ability to see into the spiritual realm is a
gift for everyone.

When the eyes of my heart are open to the unseen realm, I see...

_____

_____

_____

Living my life fully planted in Heaven means my lifestyle would become
more...

_____

_____

_____

Day 3

By Grace Through Faith

*For it is by grace you have been saved, through faith—and this
is not from yourselves, it is the gift of God.*
(Ephesians 2:8 NIV)

We are "born again" by grace through faith. The born-again salvation experience enables us to see from the heart (see John 3:3). Faith was never intended only to get us into God's family. Rather, it is the spiritual life nature. Faith sees and brings His Kingdom into focus. All of the Father's resources and benefits are accessible through faith. Remember, Jesus said He did only what He *saw* His Father do.

On a scale of 1 to 10, my measure of faith is _____ because...

_____

_____

_____

_____

Seeing from my heart bring God's Kingdom into focus, allowing me to experience...

_____

_____

_____

_____

God the Tutor

So we don't look at the troubles we can see now; rather, we fix our gaze on things that cannot be seen. For the things we see now will soon be gone, but the things we cannot see will last forever.

(2 Corinthians 4:18 NLT)

When God gives you a miracle to see and be part of, He is teaching you to see into the invisible realm. A miracle is a tutor, a gift from God to show you the spiritual side of life. After experiencing a miracle we later doubt, we haven't allowed the Lord's testimony to fully effect our thinking.

My awareness of God's Presence should be more real to me than any trouble—therefore I will gaze on...

_____

_____

_____

_____

I will fully absorb the Lord's tutoring by...

_____

_____

_____

_____

Day 4

Fix Our Eyes

So we fix our eyes not on what is seen, but on what is unseen, since what is seen is temporary, but what is unseen is eternal.

(2 Corinthians 4:18 NIV)

Kingdom thinking knows that anything is possible at any time. It's activated when we, with tender hearts, surrender to the thought patterns of God, when we receive His imaginations and say "yes." We want our minds to be full of Kingdom influence. We want miracles, and we want those miracles to have their full effect on us, changing the way we see and behave. Receiving His fullness allows Him to shape your understanding.

I long to experience the fullness of God's potential in me. I welcome Him to...

_____

_____

_____

_____

Fixing my eyes on His Presence brings me...

_____

_____

_____

_____

Day 5

Storms Calmed

...Jonah had gone below deck, where he lay down and fell into a deep sleep. The captain went to him and said, "How can you sleep? Get up and call on your god! Maybe he will take notice of us so that we will not perish."

(Jonah 1:5-6 NIV)

If we only cry out when facing a storm, we are abdicating our role in a miracle. God always provides the tools to calm the storm and brings about a miraculous result. He allows problems so we can defeat them. The tools are in the boat with us, but the enemy fans the winds of fear so we might forget about the tools.

I don't look forward to a stormy life, but being part of God's miracle makes me...

_____

_____

_____

_____

The tools in my boat include...

_____

_____

_____

_____

Day 5

Storms Conquered

*...Jonah was sound asleep down in the hold. So the captain went
down after him. "How can you sleep at a time like this?" he shouted.
"Get up and pray to your god! Maybe he will pay attention
to us and spare our lives."*

(Jonah 1:5-6 NLT)

Are you facing a storm? Have you allowed past miracles to "tutor" you to a place of faith adequate for your current challenge? Some people face storms because they took a left when God took a right. Subsequently, God allows a storm in His mercy to drive us back onto His perfect path.

God has already given me all I need to conquer every conflict, which includes (see Ephesians 6:11-17)...

_____

_____

_____

_____

Thank You, Lord, for equipping and empowering me with Your...

_____

_____

_____

_____

Rise and Give Thanks

*With my whole heart, with my whole life, and with my innermost
being, I bow in wonder and love before you, the holy God!*
(Psalm 103:1 TPT)

A tough lesson to learn is how to trust and praise God in the time between a
promise and its fulfillment. It is a powerful act of spiritual warfare to stand in
the middle of death and disease, conflict and unresolved issues, and to cause
your spirit to rise and give thanks to God—but we must declare God's goodness and faithfulness even in the midst of our trial, before we have an answer.

I will give God the gift of praise in the midst of pain, chaos, and confusion
when I...

_____

_____

_____

_____

To remain calm during a crisis, I will bow in wonder and love before You,
Lord, and...

_____

_____

_____

_____

Day 6

Praise His Holy Name

Praise the Lord, my soul; all my inmost being, praise his holy name.
(Psalm 103:1 NIV)

When stuck in conflict and uncertainty, and yet you praise Him without manipulation, it is a sacrifice that produces something beautiful—a place of entrance where the King of glory can invade your situation. That place of praise in the midst of conflict is where His Presence rests. When you move above human explanation and into a place of trust, you are in His Presence.

Because it's not natural to praise when I'm hurting or in trouble, I will practice by...

_____

_____

_____

_____

Lord, I want to be in Your Presence during all the good times and bad times—meet me there now as I face...

_____

_____

_____

_____

Day 7

God Is God

God is not a man, so he does not lie. He is not human, so he does not change his mind. Has he ever spoken and failed to act? Has he ever promised and not carried it through?
(Numbers 23:29 NLT)

When some Christians face uncertainty with no answer for their problem, they ascribe anti-biblical character traits to God. For example, they think He won't help them financially or heal them or forgive them, even though the Bible says otherwise (see Philippians 4:19 and Psalm 103:3).

Sometimes I have defined God's character by my circumstances—but no more! From now on...

_____

_____

_____

_____

God is who He says He is—the Great I Am, the Lion of Judah, the...

_____

_____

_____

_____

Day 7

The Great I Am

God said to Moses, "I AM WHO I AM." And He said, "Thus you
shall say to the children of Israel, 'I AM has sent me to you.'"
(Exodus 3:14 NKJV)

Uncertainty causes some people to deny God's true nature and embrace sickness and disease, poverty and mental anguish as "gifts" from God—that is a devastating lie from hell. It's blasphemous to attribute to God the work of the devil. But many Christians want answers so badly that they invent theological answers to make themselves feel good about their present condition. In doing so, they sacrifice the truth about God on the altar of human reasoning.

When life gets scary, I will turn toward God and praise Him for who He really is, the One who...

_____

_____

_____

_____

Human reasoning is far inferior to God's spiritual truth in these ways:

_____

_____

_____

_____

Suffering and Glory

*For I consider [from the standpoint of faith] that the sufferings
of the present life are not worthy to be compared with the glory
that is about to be revealed to us and in us!*

(Romans 8:18 AMP)

God is good all the time. The devil is bad all the time. Always remember the difference between the two! Healing, salvation, wholeness, provision, and joy have already been given to us through Christ's sacrifice. When in the middle of a conflict, rise above circumstance and declare that He is good all the time, *no matter what.* God is good—God is great!

When Jesus died on the Cross, He saved me from...

_____

_____

_____

_____

I never want to forget what Jesus' sacrifice means to me, so I will...

_____

_____

_____

_____

Day 8

Present and Future

*For I consider that the sufferings of this present time are not worthy
to be compared with the glory which shall be revealed in us.*
(Romans 8:18 NKJV)

God is good all the time and His will for healing and wholeness does not change, despite what we see in the natural. You can rest knowing that two things are guaranteed to you. First, in every situation of loss by the devourer, all things will work together for good. Second, our God is a God of vengeance. The devil never has the final say in anything.

I will use God's promises as a sword to cut down lies from the evil one—starting with the lie...

_____

_____

_____

_____

I will use God's promises as a warm blanket wrapped around me as a...

_____

_____

_____

_____

Day 9

You Are My God

O God, You are my God; early will I seek You;
my soul thirsts for You; my flesh longs for You in a dry
and thirsty land where there is no water.

(Psalm 63:1 NKJV)

King David experienced the actual, manifested Presence of God that was upon the Ark of the Covenant. God's glory radiated visibly from it, and David was immeasurably impacted by God's Presence. I don't think David was speaking purely metaphorically in Psalm 63. He was declaring that the Presence and glory of God actually affected his body that ached for Living Water.

God, I want to know You like David did and encounter You with my whole being—spirit, soul, and body, which may mean seeing You...

_____

_____

_____

_____

"O God, You are my God," and I devote myself to You in various ways including...

_____

_____

_____

_____

Day 9

My Earnest Search

O God, you are my God; I earnestly search for you. My soul thirsts for you; my whole body longs for you in this parched and weary land where there is no water.
(Psalm 63:1 NLT)

What was true for David is true for us. As we hunger for food or thirst for water, our physical bodies—not just our emotions, intellects, and spirits—can ache for God and can be satisfied by God. There is no such thing as hunger without the potential of fulfillment. God has put within our makeup the capacity to recognize Him.

Earnestly searching for God will be my new pastime! I look forward to finding Him when I look...

_____

_____

_____

_____

My hunger and thirst will be satisfied when I discover...

_____

_____

_____

_____

Day 10

Passing By

He [Jesus] saw the disciples straining at the oars, because the wind was against them. Shortly before dawn he went out to them, walking on the lake. He was about to pass by them.

(Mark 6:48 NIV)

God communicates with us in various ways—impressions of the heart, mental pictures, feelings, emotions, and physical sensations. Sometimes Jesus walks by our boat and does not intend to get in, figuratively speaking. He is within reach, but doesn't automatically step into the boat unless we ask Him to join us. If we don't perceive He's there, we miss an opportunity.

Discerning God's Presence depends largely on the Holy Spirit's help to...

_____

_____

_____

_____

I remember when I felt Jesus close by but not fully discernable. This experience left me thinking...

_____

_____

_____

_____

Perceiving God's Presence

Then He saw them straining at rowing, for the wind was against
them. Now about the fourth watch of the night He came to them,
walking on the sea, and would have passed them by.

(Mark 6:48 NKJV)

How do you know when God is close? How do you feel, sense, or perceive God when He is moving near you? You need to know the answers to fully live the normal Christian life. Without understanding that God moves and communicates with you in the physical realm, your mind cannot fully come into line with Heaven's reality.

I'm humbled knowing that God wants to communicate with me and will open myself fully to receive His Presence by...

_____

_____

_____

_____

I'm eager to learn all the unique ways I can connect with my Father and will...

_____

_____

_____

_____

_____

Day 11

Everything Belongs to You!

So don't be proud of your allegiance to any human leader. For actually, you already have everything! It has all been given for your benefit...whether it's the world or life or death, or whether it's the present or the future—everything belongs to you!
(1 Corinthians 3:21-22 TPT)

A spiritual inheritance enables the next generation to start where the previous generation left off. This is a significant yet overlooked principle in the Christian life. God wants generations to pass on their spiritual inheritances. We have inherited graces from the Lord so we don't have to go through what a previous generation went through. The same for the next generation of believers.

Father, open my eyes to all that You have given me as my inheritance. I hope and pray I see...

_____

_____

_____

_____

I want to access everything that God has for me, including...

_____

_____

_____

Day 11

Your Inheritance

So then, no more boasting about human leaders!
All things are yours, whether...the world or life or death
or the present or the future—all are yours.
(1 Corinthians 3:21-22 NIV)

A spiritual inheritance makes us more effective and efficient when representing God and His Kingdom. It's delightful and encouraging, but not simply for personal gratification. Receiving a spiritual inheritance is as if years ago somebody deposited $10 million in your bank account. You had the money all along, but now you can use it because you know the money is there and belongs to you.

How exciting to know that my spiritual inheritance is available! I'll use it to...

_____

_____

_____

_____

God's Kingdom inheritance is to bless me and glorify Him. My intent is to...

_____

_____

_____

_____

Day 12

Spiritual Footprints

So all of us who have had that veil removed can see and reflect the glory of the Lord. And the Lord—who is the Spirit—makes us more and more like him as we are changed into his glorious image.

(2 Corinthians 3:18 NLT)

So far, every generation has had to learn from scratch how to recognize God's Presence, to reflect His glory. The answer to this tragedy is our spiritual inheritance. God is serious about returning for a glorious Church—let's determine to leave behind a legacy of well-grounded spiritual footprints for future generations.

My spiritual inheritance stems from family who left behind a legacy of...

_____

_____

_____

Starting today I will live with the mindset of passing along my experiences with God's Presence—to preserve His...

_____

_____

_____

Day 12

Truth on Top of Truth

And we all, who with unveiled faces contemplate the Lord's glory, are being transformed into his image with ever-increasing glory, which comes from the Lord, who is the Spirit.

(2 Corinthians 3:18 NIV)

We with *"unveiled faces"* must understand and embrace our spiritual inheritance. We were never intended to start over from scratch every two or three generations. God wants each generation to serve at a higher level. What we take for granted today cost the previous generation tremendously. Inheritance builds truth on top of truth, allowing us to move forward into new Kingdom advancement.

I'm blessed to be part of God's family. I will honor my role by...

_____

_____

_____

_____

I will identify my spiritual ancestors _____,

honor their breakthroughs _____, and

their victories _____ will become mine.

Day 13

Every Day a Harvest Day

Don't you have a saying, "It's still four months until harvest"? I tell you, open your eyes and look at the fields! They are ripe for harvest.
(John 4:35 NIV)

We live and work by natural principles, and we understand spiritual things through natural events. Evangelism is compared to a harvest because most people are familiar with plowing a field, planting seed, watering, tending, and harvesting. In John 4:35, Jesus is saying that with a superior revelation not bounded by the natural order, every day is harvest day.

As a child of God I'm not limited by the laws of nature; therefore, I can see the fullness of my inheritance now—which is...

I will pass on my inheritance for the benefit of future generations, praying that they will...

Day 13

A Supernatural Harvestable Season

You know the saying, "Four months between planting and harvest."
But I say, wake up and look around. The fields are
already ripe for harvest.

(John 4:35 NLT)

We must wake up and look around to see from God's perspective. By revelation, you have access to an inheritance that is beyond your wildest imagination and dreams. Before Jesus returns, the redeemed will walk in their inheritance—stepping into the cumulative revelation of the whole Gospel, and having the anointing to see a supernatural season when all people are harvestable.

The Bible tells me that Heaven's authority has been released to me through Jesus Christ. With that authority, I will...

_____

_____

_____

Lord, I will obey Your command to help bring Your Kingdom upon the earth as it is in Heaven by...

_____

_____

_____

The Divine "Yes" of God

Jesus Christ is the Son of God...has never been both a "yes" and
a "no." He has always been and always will be for us
a resounding "YES!" For all of God's promises find
their "yes" of fulfillment in him...
(2 Corinthians 1:19-20 TPT)

Jesus is the Divine Yes of God, revealing the complete picture of God. Everything you know about God can be found in the person of Jesus. Jesus is the fulfillment of all of humanity's hopes and dreams. God's will on earth is not complete without His character, love, and power working in each of us who confess Him as Lord.

God, thank You for sending Your Son, the tangible revelation of Your goodness and epitomizes Your every...

_____

_____

_____

_____

My definition of "Jesus the Divine Yes of God" encompasses...

_____

_____

_____

_____

Day 14

God's Countless Promises

*For the Son of God, Jesus Christ, who was preached among you
by us...was not Yes and No, but in Him was Yes. For all the
promises of God in Him are Yes, and in Him Amen,
to the glory of God through us.*

(2 Corinthians 1:19-20 NKJV)

God has countless promises for us, and they are all yes in Jesus. He constantly overflows with words of hope and promise for His people. His grace makes it possible for us to have an effect on the outcome of matters simply through our agreement, our *amen*. When we agree with God's will and say "amen" to what God is saying in Heaven, this is divine partnership.

God has invited believers to co-labor with Him and I'm excited to work alongside Him to...

_____

_____

_____

_____

To represent God on earth means basking in His Presence as much as possible so I can genuinely...

_____

_____

_____

_____

Day 15

God Is Better Than…

*Now you [collectively] are Christ's body, and individually [you are]
members of it [each with his own special purpose and function].*
(1 Corinthians 12:27 AMP)

Make no mistake. God is capable of doing everything the Gospel requires all
on His own. Of course He can preach better, heal and deliver better, and He
is absolute perfect holiness. His love is completely unselfish, without shad-
ows and hidden agendas. His love is beyond our comprehension. He does
not need us—yet He desires us and enables us to become His dream come
true.

Father, Your desire to work with me to change the world is hard to compre-
hend and beautifully humbling. I will honor Your desire today when I…

_____

_____

_____

_____

I'd like to add to my list—God is better than…

_____

_____

_____

_____

Day 15

His Body on Earth

Now you are the body of Christ, and members individually.
(**1 Corinthians 12:27 NKJV**)

We are what God dreamed of in eternity past—the body of Christ on earth. Jesus is the Head of His Church, the body. To think any other way ultimately undermines our purpose in this life. God made no mistakes. He never wanted a different person for this exact moment in time other than you, experiencing the fullest expression of yourself. He wants you to trust Him and find yourself in Him.

This evening I open my heart, mind, and spirit to hear from my heavenly Father, listening for Him to tell me who I truly am and His plans for me. What He tells me I will write here:

_____

_____

_____

_____

_____

_____

_____

_____

Day 16

Perfect Unity

You live fully in me and now I live fully in them so that they will experience perfect unity, and the world will be convinced that you have sent me, for they will see that you love each one of them with the same passionate love that you have for me.

(John 17:23 TPT)

Much of today's Gospel teachings are aimed at satisfying the needs and desires of an individual believer. That's not necessarily wrong; it's just dangerously incomplete. Some things are too precious for God to give to only one person. They must be imparted to a body of believers; otherwise, the temptation for pride will become the beast that devours.

I prefer meeting with God one on one when I am...

_____

_____

_____

_____

I prefer meeting with God in the company of others when I am...

_____

_____

_____

_____

Day 16

So the World Will Know

*I in them, and You in Me; that they may be made perfect in one,
and that the world may know that You have sent Me, and
have loved them as You have loved Me.*

(John 17:23 NKJV)

Scriptures say *our* Father, not *my* Father. And, *we* have the mind of Christ, not *I* have the mind of Christ. And He is returning for a spotless bride (body), not a spotless individual. The list goes on in this regard. The Gospel is not a personal cure-all. It must affect individual believers—to bring ultimate transformation to the world.

I admit I'm guilty of hoarding God's blessings for myself rather than…

_____

_____

_____

_____

I'm sorry for not sharing more of the Good News with more of…

_____

_____

_____

_____

Transformation

Declare His glory among the nations, His wonders among all people.
(Psalm 96:3 NKJV)

The transformation of society starts with the transformation of the mind of an individual. It begins with the one. The acorn becomes a tree that produces a forest. A transformed mind transforms a person who transforms a city. And transformed cities effect a nation, bringing about a reformation. This is the heart of God.

Help me to expand my vision, Holy Spirit! Fill me with Your dreams for my family, my city, my nation, and...

_____

_____

_____

_____

The wonders I will declare among all people are...

_____

_____

_____

_____

Tell Everyone

Publish his glorious deeds among the nations.
Tell everyone about the amazing things he does.

(Psalm 96:3 NLT)

Jesus didn't go through everything He went through so we could just "do church" until He returned. He still delivers people, cities, and nations from sin and disease. It's time for the brilliance of our renewed minds to take center stage. We cannot allow ourselves to be overcome with the hopelessness that prevails in these uncertain days. It's time to publish His glorious deeds and tell everyone about Him!

I am ready to tell the world who God is and all that He has done in my life to deliver me from...

_____

_____

_____

_____

God's Presence enters into every environment and fills the atmosphere when I obey His Word to tell others that He...

_____

_____

_____

_____

Day 18

So None Will Perish

The Lord is not slack concerning His promise, as some count slackness,
but is longsuffering toward us, not willing that any should perish
but that all should come to repentance.

(2 Peter 3:9 NKJV)

Our mistake is often seen when we create explanations to tragedies and difficulties that God is not causing. This kind of reasoning appeals to the minds of those who have not yet settled into a lifestyle that treasures mystery. Mystery is as important as revelation. Strangely, the sovereignty of God is the one carpet that most unanswered questions get swept under. The sovereignty of God is one of the most valuable truths in Scripture. Perhaps this is why the enemy works so hard to pervert it.

Reflect on this prayer: God, help me to hold a space for Your mystery in my thinking. Help me to never minimize or explain away who You are in an effort to protect myself.

Lord, I repent right now of thinking wrongly about…

Day 18

EVENING

Repentance

The Lord isn't really being slow about his promise, as some people think. No, he is being patient for your sake. He does not want anyone to be destroyed, but wants everyone to repent.

(2 Peter 3:9 NLT)

Some things God will do with or without us. And some things will not get done if we don't do our part. For example, Jesus is going to return whether we vote yes or no. It is established. On the other hand, He doesn't want anyone to be destroyed. But without our preaching repentance, it won't happen—even though it's God's will.

God is sovereign, yet He chose to partner with humans to reveal His nature. My role in that partnership is to...

_____

_____

_____

_____

Speaking to someone about repentance is hard for me because...

_____

_____

_____

_____

Day 19

Heaven on Earth

Your kingdom come, your will be done, on earth as it is in heaven.

(Matthew 6:10 NIV)

It's a painful realization, but seldom does it feel like Heaven on earth when we step into many of today's churches. For His will to be fully realized starts with embracing the supreme value of Heaven—His Presence. Everything is attached to the Presence of the Lord, which in biblical language means His face. The regard for the Presence of God must have practical application for church life for us to have His intended will to be done here on earth.

Longing for God's Presence above all else causes me to...

_____

_____

_____

_____

I will keep God's face always in front of me, forever my first priority, which means I will...

_____

_____

_____

_____

Day 19

The Reality Within

Your kingdom come. Your will be done on earth as it is in heaven.
(Matthew 6:10 NKJV)

God gave us both permission and a command to allow His world to shape our world here on earth. But there is no transformation of the world *around* us if there is no transformation of the world *within* us. That is both good news and bad, depending on our heart issues. Discovering His will should fill our days with possibility-thinking, not thinking focused on evil or calamity.

God created me to be a dreamer, a problem-solver, a creator like Him. Keeping me back from living that lifestyle include...

_____

_____

_____

_____

God isn't surprised by the darkness in the world—His light is always shining. Have I allowed His light in me to dim?

_____

_____

_____

_____

Day 20

Flavorful

You are the salt of the earth; but if the salt loses its flavor, how shall it be seasoned? It is then good for nothing but to be thrown out and trampled underfoot....

(Matthew 5:13 NKJV)

Jesus says we are the salt of the earth and add flavor to life. But if we, the Church, keep to ourselves, hoping the world will find their way into our meetings and embrace our values, we are salt that is "good for nothing." We must be sprinkled into the systems of this world to have full effect—the transformation of the world around us.

Jesus, I pray for the wisdom and the courage to bring flavor to the world with my...

_____

_____

_____

_____

Being "salty" has many meanings in the secular and the spiritual world. My definition is...

_____

_____

_____

_____

Day 20

Flavorless

You are the salt of the earth. But what good is salt if it has lost its
flavor? Can you make it salty again? It will be thrown
out and trampled underfoot as worthless.

(Matthew 5:13 NLT)

Our role includes living a holy life, being filled with compassion, and demonstrating His power. But wisdom must be added to bring about God's purposes on earth. We are to become the servants of all, bringing the flavor of His wisdom into this world so people can see and taste His kindness—leading to repentance (see Romans 2:4).

Looking back over my day, were my interactions filled with holy affection for my family, coworkers, strangers?

_____

_____

_____

_____

God's kindness leads people to a change of heart. Am I naturally kind, or do I need to refine that aspect of my personality?

_____

_____

_____

_____

_____

Day 21

From Servants to Friends

*I no longer call you servants, because a servant does not know his
master's business. Instead, I have called you friends, for everything
that I learned from my Father I have made known to you.*

(John 15:15 NIV)

Toward the end of His earthly life, Jesus gave His disciples the ultimate
promotion—to be His friends. Jesus brought them into His life. With this
promotion, the disciples' attention would shift from the task at hand to the
One within reach—Jesus. They were given access to the secrets in God's
heart through their personal relationship with His Son.

Jesus is the ultimate Best Friend! What a blessing and privilege to be close to
Him and share...

_____

_____

_____

_____

I enjoy spending time with my friends—especially Jesus because we...

_____

_____

_____

_____

Day 21

His Confidant

*I no longer call you slaves, because a master doesn't confide in his
slaves. Now you are my friends, since I have told
you everything the Father told me.*

(John 15:15 NLT)

Jesus told His disciples that slaves or servants are task-oriented. Obedience is their primary focus. But friends have a different focus. Friends are more concerned about disappointing, than disobeying. The disciples' focus shifted from the commandments to His Presence, from the assignment to relationship. Their friendship with Jesus makes His Presence with us possible.

How many true confidants do I have in my life right now? Jesus is the very best Confidant I will ever have because I trust Him with knowing...

_____

_____

_____

_____

Over the years, friends have come and gone during various seasons—but Jesus is the Friend who...

_____

_____

_____

_____

Day 22

Worried and Troubled

And Jesus answered and said to her, "Martha, Martha, you are worried and troubled about many things. But one thing is needed, and Mary has chosen that good part, which will not be taken away from her."
(Luke 10:41-42 NKJV)

Paradigm shifts take place as we embrace being God's friends. First, *what we know* changes as we gain access to the heart of the Father. Second, our *experiences* change to becoming intimate encounters. Third, our *function* radically changes from working *for* Him to working *with* Him. Fourth, our *identity* is profoundly transformed, setting the tone for all we do and become.

Father, help me to truly understand who I am in You. I'm listening...

_____

_____

_____

_____

As Mary did, I choose the *"good part,"* which I believe to be...

_____

_____

_____

_____

Day 22

Choose What Is Better

"Martha, Martha," the Lord answered, "you are worried and upset
about many things, but few things are needed—or indeed
only one. Mary has chosen what is better, and it
will not be taken away from her."
(Luke 10:41-42 NIV)

The Mary and Martha story exposes the difference between servants and friends. Mary chose to sit at Jesus' feet while Martha chose to work in the kitchen. To say we need both Marys and Marthas misses the point entirely. Mary wasn't a non-worker; she just learned to serve from His Presence. Working *from* His Presence is better than working *for* His Presence.

I've considered myself as a Mary/Martha (circle one), not a Mary/Martha (circle one) because I...

_____

_____

_____

_____

Working *from* His Presence changes the way I think about...

_____

_____

_____

_____

_____

Day 23

MORNING

Rejoicing in His Presence

When he gave the sea its boundary...and when he marked out the foundations of the earth. Then I was constantly at his side. I was filled with delight day after day, rejoicing always in his presence.

(Proverbs 8:29-30 NIV)

Wisdom and creativity are related subjects in the Bible. In fact, creativity is a manifestation of wisdom in the context of excellence and integrity. Wisdom is personified in Proverbs 8 and is the companion of God at the creation of all things. Both are essential tools needed to be an effective witness to those who don't know God. Wisdom makes our role in this world desirable to seekers.

The phrase "creativity is a manifestation of wisdom" brings to mind...

_____

_____

_____

_____

I will be creative and wise as I witness to _____ the next time I see him/her, saying that...

_____

_____

_____

_____

Day 23

Daily His Delight

*When He assigned to the sea its limit...He marked out the
foundations of the earth, then I was beside Him as a master
craftsman; and I was daily His delight, rejoicing always before Him.*
(Proverbs 8:29-30 NKJV)

The six days of creation saw the most wonderful display of wisdom and art imaginable. As God spoke, light and beauty, sound and color, all flowed together seamlessly as wisdom set the world's boundaries. Wisdom is the *"master craftsman."* We were born to partner with wisdom—to live in it and display it through creative expression.

God's creativity amazes me every day—from diverse animals and flowers to...

_____

_____

_____

_____

With the Holy Spirit's help, I would love to explore wisdom's workmanship that God planted in my heart so I could...

_____

_____

_____

_____

MORNING

Spirit-Filled Workmanship

And I have filled him with the Spirit of God, in wisdom, in understanding, in knowledge, and in all manner of workmanship.

(Exodus 31:3 NKJV)

Bezalel is the first person filled with the Spirit of God in Scripture. His assignment was to build a house where God would dwell among His people. God revealed what the house should look like, and gave Bezalel supernatural wisdom to complete the task with artistic excellence. Wisdom qualified him as an artisan to design and build what was in God's heart.

I need Your wisdom, Father, to run after the dreams in my heart; fill me today with Your creative and wise Spirit so I can...

_____

_____

_____

_____

The dreams in my heart consist of...

_____

_____

_____

_____

Day 24

Filled with the Spirit

I have filled him with the Spirit of God, giving him great wisdom,
ability, and expertise in all kinds of crafts.
(Exodus 31:3 NLT)

Wisdom characteristics include artistic design, excellence, and inventive work—part of what being filled with the Spirit looked like in Moses' day. The New Testament adds power, accessing the miracle realm through the Holy Spirit—produces wise believers making practical contributions to society, confronting impossibilities through the Cross, and solving problems with miracles, signs, and wonders. All this is the balanced Christian life.

Tomorrow I will pay attention to what frustrates me, and then I'll ask God to reveal His supernaturally creative solutions. I'll start with my frustration about...

_____

_____

_____

_____

Then I'll go on to my frustration about...

_____

_____

_____

_____

Day 25

Don't Hide Your Light

So don't hide your light! Let it shine brightly before others, so that the commendable things you do will shine as light upon them, and then they will give their praise to your Father in heaven.
(Matthew 5:16 TPT)

Many people feel disqualified because they confine creativity to art and music. Everyone has some measure of creativity, which should be consistently expressed throughout life. Creativity doesn't always mean making or doing something new or different. Most great ideas are offsprings of other concepts. Wisdom can build on an everyday item or concept to create something new and better.

I haven't had the courage to be creative—yet I've always wanted to try my hand at...

_____

_____

_____

_____

And I've always wanted to _____ but thought it was too...

_____

_____

_____

_____

EVENING

Let Your Light Shine

*In the same way, let your light shine before others, that they may see
your good deeds and glorify your Father in heaven.*
(Matthew 5:16 NIV)

A misconception is that creativity must come from pain. It's true that some
of the greatest works of art came from people who were troubled or experienced tragedies. It often does take trauma to launch people into seeing life's
true priorities. Believers don't need that experience. Having our old nature
crucified with Christ is the only tragedy needed to launch us into our proper
roles of creative influence.

Trouble and/or tragedy has affected my creative influence in the following
ways...

_____

_____

_____

Lord, may Your Presence provoke me to do good deeds for others that will
glorify You; my good deeds will include...

_____

_____

_____

_____

Dreaming Dreams

Before you do anything, put your trust totally in God and not in yourself. Then every plan you make will succeed.
(Proverbs 16:3 TPT)

Many believers become discouraged when they think their dreams fail. In pain and frustration, they forget they have the right to dream. But here's a higher reality—unfilled dreams for one person actually prepares the way for others who carry the same dream to eventually experience breakthrough. It is hard to take comfort in this because we usually think it's all about us—it's not. There is no failure in faith.

Father, bring to mind moments when I've felt failure. Please show me how You see it—and I'll write what You tell me here:

_____

_____

_____

_____

What dreams do I need to resurrect?

_____

_____

_____

_____

Setting the Stage

Commit to the Lord whatever you do,
and he will establish your plans.

(Proverbs 16:3 NIV)

Often a tragic loss on earth is viewed quite differently in Heaven. What is honored in Heaven is frequently pitied or mocked on earth. To our detriment, we have lived without the consciousness that a failed attempt at a dream often becomes the foundation of another person's success. Some water, others plant, and still others harvest. You have an important role to set the stage for the King of kings to receive more glory. It's all about *Him.*

A loss can overwhelm me—next time I will view it from Heaven's perspective by...

_____

_____

_____

_____

When I feel defeated, I will go directly into God's Presence and listen for His voice saying...

_____

_____

_____

_____

Day 27

Who Does He Think He Is?

Everyone was impressed by how well Jesus spoke...But they were surprised at his presumption to speak as a prophet, so they said among themselves, "Who does he think he is? This is Joseph's son, who grew up here in Nazareth."

(Luke 4:22 TPT)

An intellectual Gospel is always in danger of creating a god who looks like us—is our size. Living with mystery is the privilege of our walk with Christ. The walk of faith is to live according to the revelation we have received in the midst of the mysteries we can't explain.

I need to expand my vision of God—go past my logical understanding by...

_____

_____

_____

_____

Who in my life may be speaking what I need to hear, yet I dismiss it because...

_____

_____

_____

_____

Day 27

Q & A

Everyone spoke well of him and was amazed by the gracious words that came from his lips. "How can this be?" they asked. "Isn't this Joseph's son?"

(Luke 4:22 NLT)

Not understanding is okay. Restricting our spiritual life to what we understand is not. It is immaturity at best. Such a controlling spirit is destructive to the development of a Christlike nature. God responds to faith but will not surrender to our demands for control. Maturity requires a heartfelt embrace of what we do not understand as an essential expression of faith.

I have a lot of questions about a lot of things. I will take each one to my heavenly Father and trust that His answers will...

_____

_____

_____

_____

My first question is...

_____

_____

_____

_____

Living in Compromise

*And without faith it is impossible to please God, because anyone who
comes to him must believe that he exists and that he
rewards those who earnestly seek him.*

(Hebrews 11:6 NIV)

We can easily obey when God gives us understanding—it's not as easy when
facing questions and circumstances that seem to contradict what we understand. We mistakenly bring the Bible down to our level of experience to feel
better about living in compromise—a compromise of Scripture revelation.
We must bring our lifestyle up to the standard of God's Word.

I will bring my lifestyle up to the level of faith revealed in the Scriptures
when I depend on...

_____

_____

_____

_____

God's direction is clear when I fully trust Him to...

_____

_____

_____

_____

Living in Revelation

*It is impossible to please God without faith. Anyone who wants to
come to him must believe that God exists and that
he rewards those who sincerely seek him.*

(Hebrews 11:6 NLT)

Embracing revelation with one hand and mystery with the other forms a
perfect cross—a cross that everyone who is hungry to do the works of Jesus
will have to carry. God must violate our logic to invite us away from the
deception of relying on our own reasoning. With faith, we must believe God
exists—which pleases Him. Our rewards? Revelations to stretch our minds
and hearts. Open both to God's wondrous blessings this evening before clos-
ing your eyes to rest.

To stretch my mind I will...

_____

_____

_____

_____

To stretch my heart I will...

_____

_____

_____

_____

MORNING

God's Peace

And the peace of God, which surpasses all understanding, will guard your hearts and minds through Christ Jesus.
(Philippians 4:7 NKJV)

Our spirit is where the Holy Spirit dwells—it is alive and well and ready to receive from God. The peace of God goes beyond our understanding and positions us to renew our minds and open our hearts. If we learn more about the actual voice and Presence of the Lord, we will stop being so paranoid about being deceived by what we can't explain.

Jesus, help my spirit to rise up and take its rightful place of leadership over my mind and body. I will watch for Your Presence...

_____

_____

_____

_____

Holy Spirit, I give You my heart and will feel Your Presence when...

_____

_____

_____

_____

Hearts and Minds

Then you will experience God's peace, which exceeds anything we can understand. His peace will guard your hearts and minds as you live in Christ Jesus.

(Philippians 4:7 NLT)

Your heart can embrace what your head can't. Your heart will lead you where your logic would never dare to go. Courage rises up from within and influences the mind. In the same way, true faith affects the mind. Faith does not come from understanding—it comes from the heart. You don't believe because you understand—you understand because you believe. You'll know when your mind is truly renewed because the impossible will look logical.

God has designed me to respond to His Presence, to yield to His voice—therefore, I will...

_____

_____

_____

_____

I believe; I have faith; I understand; I...

_____

_____

_____

_____

Day 30

Made Holy
Once and for All

By God's will we have been purified and made holy once and for all
through the sacrifice of the body of Jesus, the Messiah!
(Hebrews 10:10 TPT)

A yielded imagination becomes a sanctified imagination, which is positioned to receive godly visions and dreams. There is paranoia over the use of the imagination in Western world churches. As a result, unbelievers often lead the way in creative expression—through the arts and inventions—as they have no bias against imagination. Believers have been purified and made holy—once and for all. This we must believe regarding all aspects of our lives.

I repent for limiting my imagination because of fear or a religious spirit. In light of my newfound freedom, I will...

God, inspire my imagination—give me daydreams...

Made Holy Once for All Time

God's will was for us to be made holy by the sacrifice of the body of Jesus Christ, once for all time.

(Hebrews 10:10 NLT)

God would love to use our imagination to paint His impressions and will in our lives. However, if we are preoccupied with "not being worthy," we are too self-centered to be trusted with much revelation. It has to stop being about us long enough to realize we have been made holy through Christ's sacrifice. We have unlimited access to the mysteries of God, revealed by our imaginations, to touch the needs of a dying world.

I must settle into the foundation of God's love so that together we can build...

_____

_____

_____

_____

I will co-labor with God to release the Kingdom into this broken world with our...

_____

_____

_____

_____

Day 31

All Authority

*And Jesus came and spoke to them, saying, "All authority
has been given to Me in heaven and on earth."*
(Matthew 28:18 NKJV)

We have been given authority; first given to us by God in Genesis (see Genesis 1:28-29), and restored to us by Jesus after His resurrection. Kingdom authority is the authority to set people free from torment and disease, to destroy the works of darkness. It moves Heaven's resources through creative expression to meet human need. It brings Heaven to earth—the authority to serve.

Father, my heart breaks for the brokenness I see around me—I ask You to help me...

_____

_____

_____

_____

Help me to step into the authority You gave me so I can see Your heart and...

_____

_____

_____

_____

Not Some—All Authority

*Jesus came and told his disciples, "I have been given all
authority in heaven and on earth."*
(Matthew 28:18 NLT)

As with most Kingdom principles, the truths of humanity's dominion and authority are dangerous in the hands of those who desire to rule over others. These concepts seem to validate some people's selfishness. But when these truths are expressed through the humble servant, the world is rocked to its core. Becoming servants to this world is the key to open the doors of possibility that are generally thought of as closed or forbidden.

Becoming a servant to the world means that I must...

_____

_____

_____

_____

I will use the authority that Jesus died to give me by...

_____

_____

_____

_____

Trusted with Much

Whoever can be trusted with very little can also be trusted with much, and whoever is dishonest with very little will also be dishonest with much.

(Luke 16:10 NIV)

There is no such thing as secular employment—after we are born again, everything about us is redeemed for Kingdom purposes. It's all spiritual. It's either a legitimate Kingdom expression, or we shouldn't be involved. Every believer is in full-time ministry—our pulpits are either in the church or in the world's marketplaces. Be sure to preach only good news. And when necessary, use words!

Lord, open my eyes to see opportunities to express Your Kingdom, whether I'm at _____ or in _____.

_____

_____

_____

_____

I will destroy every box I may have placed around Your Presence—help me share Your heart with...

_____

_____

_____

_____

EVENING

Greater Responsibilities

If you are faithful in little things, you will be faithful in large ones.
But if you are dishonest in little things, you won't
be honest with greater responsibilities.

(Luke 16:10 NLT)

The call of God is important, not because of a title—because of the One who called. A call to be in business or a wife and mother is as valuable in the Kingdom as is an evangelist or missionary. Eternal rewards are based on our faithfulness to what God has given and called us to be and to do. Honor must be given to those faithful in God's calling, no matter what it is.

God has infused the world with diversity on purpose—and my calling mean a lot to Him because...

_____

_____

_____

_____

A diverse world expresses God's multifaceted nature. I'm part of that diversity as a...

_____

_____

_____

_____

MORNING

Expressing Love

Beloved ones, God has called us to live a life of freedom in the Holy Spirit. ...Freedom means that we become so completely free of self-indulgence that we become servants of one another, expressing love in all we do.

(Galatians 5:13 TPT)

Godly ministry is to transform society by invading the world's systems to serve others. As someone said, "We shouldn't try to be the best *in* the world. We should try to be the best *for* the world!" Setting aside religious agendas to make others a success is having a Kingdom mindset and makes us part of the transformation movement.

Jesus, help me see the practical, felt needs of my family, city, and nation so I can...

_____

_____

_____

_____

As Your hands and feet, Jesus, I will release Your love on earth by...

_____

_____

_____

_____

Day 33

Freedom to Serve

*You, my brothers and sisters, were called to be free. But do not use
your freedom to indulge the flesh; rather,
serve one another humbly in love.*

(Galatians 5:13 NIV)

Most churches serve the community—but sometimes with well-meaning spiritual agendas. It may sound blasphemous, but serving simply to get people saved is a religious agenda. As pure and noble as it may seem to believers, it is manipulative to the world and is viewed as impure service. The world can smell it a mile away. Serving for the benefit of others is the kind of a servant that the world welcomes.

I will pray for my church leaders—that motives and agendas will be based on servanthood and...

_____

_____

_____

_____

I will serve in ways that reveal God's kindness and...

_____

_____

_____

_____

Day 34

God—Life's First Priority

May all those who seek You [as life's first priority] rejoice and be
glad in You; May those who love Your salvation
say continually, "Let God be magnified!"

(Psalm 70:4 AMP)

Perhaps you've heard it said, "God is number one, the family is number two, and the Church is number three." That unofficial list is important, but has become confused through the years. As good as this list is, it isn't technically accurate. When God is number one, there is no number two or three—because with Him as our very top priority, everything else falls into place.

Because You are my first priority, God, I know the rest of my life will...

_____

_____

_____

_____

I can pursue what's on my heart, knowing God is my main focus...

_____

_____

_____

_____

Day 34

God Is Love

Whoever does not love does not know God, because God is love.
(1 John 4:8 NIV)

Out of our love for God, we love our family. In knowing and loving God, we can release supernatural love that is unattainable apart from God. Anyone completely abandoned to God can love others more than they thought possible. Our love for God is our love for life, which cannot be separated. God is number one, the only One.

Loving others isn't always as easy for me as it should be as...

_____

_____

_____

_____

My prayer this evening is to be bold enough to share God's passion for others: Dear Father...

_____

_____

_____

_____

Love and Liars

Whoever claims to love God yet hates a brother or sister is a liar. For whoever does not love their brother and sister, whom they have seen, cannot love God, whom they have not seen.

(1 John 4:20 NIV)

Passion for God gives birth to a passion for others. When we love God, it will be measurable by our love for people. This is such an absolute principle that God says if we don't love others, we don't actually love Him. In the wake of our passion for God and others, we prove and manifest our love for God.

Help me, God, to love well every person You place before me. Thank You for...

_____

_____

_____

_____

Help me to love those closest to me with Your patient consistency. I am grateful for...

_____

_____

_____

_____

Day 35

Love and Hate

If someone says, "I love God," but hates a fellow believer,
that person is a liar; for if we don't love people we can see,
how can we love God, whom we cannot see?

(1 John 4:20 NLT)

The key point confronting a religious mindset is that it dismisses everything not considered "sacred." The effort to accomplish the goal of loving God with no other passions creates a monastic—reclusive—lifestyle to survive. While I admire many monastic believers of the past, it is not the model Jesus gave us. The way we steward the rest of life becomes the litmus test that demonstrates an authentic love for God.

To know God, to truly share His heart, is to share His love for the world. I do that when I...

_____

_____

_____

_____

Jesus loved all people—I choose to do so as well, sharing His devotion with...

_____

_____

_____

_____

Day 36

Delight in the Lord

Take delight in the Lord, and he will give you your heart's desires.
(Psalm 37:4 NLT)

Most people have a prayer list representing our basic desires and needs, and for those we love. If not written on paper, the list is at least written in our hearts. The list includes prayers of eternal significance—salvation, healing, etc. And there's an "It would be nice" section. But sometimes God bypasses all of those and goes directly to the "I haven't even bothered to ask" part that dwells somewhere deep as the desires of our hearts.

God, thank You for the delights that You sprinkle throughout my day—the desires that I don't pray specifically about—but You fulfill them anyway, such as...

_____

_____

_____

_____

Holy Spirit, thank You for every opportunity to celebrate Your goodness—known and unknown to me...

_____

_____

_____

_____

Day 36

Your Heart's Desire

*Take delight in the Lord, and he will give
you the desires of your heart.*

(Psalm 37:4 NIV)

When God bypasses all of our prayers that have eternal significance and answers something temporal and seemingly insignificant, it can be confusing. He wants to teach us that if something matters to us, it matters to Him. His bypassing our "urgent" and "it would be nice" prayers, and entering the secret desires of the heart list reveals more about our heavenly Father than answering whatever we've been praying about.

This evening, Lord, I open my heart and my prayer list to You, knowing your answers will be...

_____

_____

_____

I will try not to focus so much on my "big prayers" that I miss Your precious heart-desires answers...

_____

_____

_____

Day 37

Live from Heaven to Earth

Yes, feast on all the treasures of the heavenly realm and fill your thoughts with heavenly realities, and not with the distractions of the natural realm. Your crucifixion with Christ has severed the tie to this life, and now your true life is hidden away in God in Christ.
(Colossians 3:2-3 TPT)

When we live conscious of Heaven and eternity, it radically increases our measure of impact on society. It's quite amazing that those who see Heaven most clearly have little desire for this world, yet they have the greatest impact on the world around them.

Holy Spirit, cause the reality of Heaven to be on my mind at all times so I can...

_____

_____

_____

_____

When tangled up in the fears and pains of this world...

_____

_____

_____

_____

EVENING

Think about Heaven

Think about the things of heaven, not the things of earth. For you died to this life, and your real life is hidden with Christ in God.

(Colossians 3:2-3 NLT)

The abundant life Jesus promised to His disciples is found in the unseen spiritual realm, where He displayed miracles and various supernatural expressions. We must access His world to change this one. For now, you live in two worlds, but these two realities are not to be equally prominent. You have been crucified and resurrected with Christ, seated with Him in Heaven.

I am to live from Heaven to earth, from provision to lack, from solutions to problems, and...

_____

_____

_____

_____

Heaven my lens, homeland, and native language. Earth is my target to...

_____

_____

_____

_____

Day 38

Deepening Intimacy

I pray that the Father of glory...would impart to you the riches of the Spirit of wisdom and the Spirit of revelation to know him through your deepening intimacy with him.
(Ephesians 1:17 TPT)

Changing the course of world history is our assignment. Yet we have gone as far as we can with what we presently know. We need signs that point us to something greater—the exit. We don't need signs when we travel on familiar roads. But when we're going where we've never gone before, we need signs to get there. These signs restore the wonder of the destiny.

I can step out into the unknown, trusting His signs will appear...

_____

_____

_____

_____

Never leave home without it—God's wisdom and revelation—which leads to...

_____

_____

_____

_____

Day 38

Passionately Pursued

That the God of our Lord Jesus Christ, the Father of glory, may give to you the spirit of wisdom and revelation in the knowledge of Him.
(Ephesians 1:17 NKJV)

Even a church in revival known for great teaching and citywide impact, needs more revelation. To say, "The Spirit of God is welcome here" is not enough. Many of the things we need and long for must be prayed for specifically. Only when wisdom and revelation are passionately pursued do they reside in the Christian life. These are the safeguards from succumbing to the peril of religion.

My definition of the "peril of religion" is...

_____

_____

_____

_____

I will stay hungry for more of God's Presence, and I will never regret pursuing Him...

_____

_____

_____

_____

MORNING

Words of Life

The word of God is living and powerful, and sharper than any two-edged sword, piercing even to the division of soul and spirit, and of joints and marrow, and is a discerner of the thoughts and intents of the heart.

(Hebrews 4:12 NKJV)

God's Word, the Holy Bible, is living and powerful. The ability to hear God, especially from His Word, is mandatory to enter our divine purpose and true creative expression. Our yielded hearts are impressionable as we study Scripture and receive God's revelations easily. Within that sort of tender soil, the Lord plants the seeds of Kingdom perspective that grow into global transformation.

When You stir up my passion for Your Scriptures, God, I can...

_____

_____

_____

_____

My prayer is to absorb God's Word daily, receive life from it, and encounter...

_____

_____

_____

_____

Alive and Active

For the word of God is alive and active. ...judges
the thoughts and attitudes of the heart.
(Hebrews 4:12 NIV)

The insights and empowering nature of God's Word, the Scriptures, provide solutions applicable to every society and culture. The Bible is limitless in scope, timeless, and complete, containing answers to every human dilemma. Studying Scriptures must take us beyond the historical setting, beyond language studies, and at times beyond the context and intent of the human authors. It's time to hear from God afresh—pray that His Word would once again become the living Word in our experience in His Presence.

Sometimes I skip my daily reading of God's Word. When that happens, I feel...

_____

_____

_____

_____

When I'm reading the Bible, I feel so close to God—His Presence...

_____

_____

_____

_____

Day 40

In the Beginning

In the beginning was the Word, and the Word was
with God, and the Word was God.

(John 1:1 NKJV)

God is still speaking, but everything we hear must be consistent with what He has spoken to us in His Word, the Bible. In light of burning convictions, standards and traditions have been instituted by the church for our protection—that practically suck the life and impact out of God's living Word. Though not the original intent, but it has been an unintended result.

Do I make it a practice of measuring what I hear against God's anointed Word? Why don't I? Have I been led astray intentionally? Unintentionally?

_____

_____

_____

_____

Holy Spirit, please help me internalize Scriptures so well that the Word of God is constantly in my heart and spirit. That way I can assure...

_____

_____

_____

_____

Day 40

God Was and Is Forever

*In the beginning was the Word, and the Word was
with God, and the Word was God.*

(John 1:1 NIV)

Being unaware of God's Presence costs us dearly, especially when approaching Scripture. King David authored and sang songs of his love for God's Word, and "set" the Lord before himself daily. He was conscious of God's nearness and lived from that mindset. Our sanctified imagination enables us to tap into true reality. Since I can't imagine a place where God isn't, I imagine Him with me.

This evening before I fall asleep, I will imagine God beside me and how His Presence is...

_____

_____

_____

_____

When I realize that God is closer to me than my every breath, that true reality overwhelms...

_____

_____

_____

_____

Day 41

Led by the Spirit

For those who are led by the Spirit of God are the children of God.
(Romans 8:14 NIV)

To value the Scriptures above the Holy Spirit is idolatry. It is not Father, Son, and Holy Bible; it's the Father, Son, and Holy Spirit. The Bible reveals God but is itself not God. It does not contain Him. God is bigger than His book. We are reliant on the Holy Spirit to reveal what is contained on the pages of Scripture because without Him it is a closed book.

Holy Spirit, please guide me through the Scriptures. Start today by leading me to a relevant passage that will help me deal with...

_____

_____

_____

_____

Holy Spirit, help me to encounter You in new ways that may take me out of my "comfort zone"...

_____

_____

_____

_____

The Spirit of God

For all who are led by the Spirit of God are children of God.
(Romans 8:14 NLT)

Dependency on the Holy Spirit must be more than a token prayer asking for guidance before a Bible study. We are to have an ongoing relationship with the third Person of the Trinity that affects every aspect of life. The Holy Spirit is the power of Heaven within us and eagerly reveals His mysteries to all who are truly hungry. Caution: Sinning against the Holy Spirit has eternal consequences (see Ephesians 4:30).

God gave believers not only His Son, but also His Spirit—to teach, comfort, empower, and guide us. I honor the Trinity when I...

_____

_____

_____

_____

Even Abraham, Moses, and David didn't have God's Spirit living inside them. For His indwelling Spirit I am thankful and...

_____

_____

_____

_____

Day 42

God's Good Spirit

*You also gave Your good Spirit to instruct them, and did
not withhold Your manna from their mouth,
and gave them water for their thirst.*
(Nehemiah 9:20 NKJV)

Doctrine must be kept supple with the oil of the Spirit. If rigid and unmoving, it will not yield to God's habit of opening more of His Word to us. God loves to add to our knowledge things we think we already understand. Too much rigidity bursts our doctrinal wineskins with the weight of ongoing revelation. The end result is the church becomes irrelevant and powerless to the surrounding world.

Father, forgive me for any area in my life where I have grown stiff against the move of...

_____

_____

_____

_____

I yield every structure, assumption, and design of my own at God's feet, for Him to...

_____

_____

_____

_____

The Good Spirit Instructs

You gave your good Spirit to instruct them. You did not withhold
your manna from their mouths, and you gave
them water for their thirst.

(Nehemiah 9:20 NIV)

The Holy Spirit has to be free to speak to us about what is on His heart—especially what we naturally resist. We must be open to truth when it has a biblical basis and is accompanied by the breath of God making it come alive for a specific purpose. The error is building a theological monument around a particular point of view that conveniently excludes certain portions of Scripture to help us feel secure in a doctrinal bent. Too often human structures exclude the move of God's Spirit.

I don't want to exclude the move of God's Spirit in any way. Precautions I will take are...

_____

_____

_____

_____

To stay flexible to feeling and hearing God's Presence, I will stay rooted in...

_____

_____

_____

_____

Day 43

Pay Attention

So above all, guard the affections of your heart, for they affect all that you are. Pay attention to the welfare of your innermost being, for from there flows the wellspring of life.
(Proverbs 4:23 TPT)

Biblical meditation is a completely different from what is encouraged in the New Age culture. Theirs is a counterfeit because it encourages people to empty their minds. True Christian meditation encourages people to fill their hearts, spirits, and minds with God's Word, the Bible. That pure and absolute foundation takes people on an eternal journey—including daily personal interactions with the Holy Spirit.

Beginning today I will pay attention to...

_____

_____

_____

Feasting on the Scriptures trains my mind to the truth. May I have a new hunger each time I open His Word and find...

_____

_____

_____

Day 43

Guard Your Heart

Guard your heart above all else,
for it determines the course of your life.
(Proverbs 4:23 NLT)

Whatever your heart is set on when reading the Bible determines what you see. Those with evil in their hearts will misread Scripture to confirm their intent. The problem is not the method or approach to the Bible; it is whether or not we are willing to stay humble, honest, and hungry before the Lord. Keeping a pure heart makes reading God's Word a most pleasurable and spiritually uplifting journey where nothing is impossible.

When reading God's Word, I will leave behind fears of inadequacy and open my heart and spirit to receive...

_____

_____

_____

_____

I will treasure the Scriptures, knowing His Spirit feeds me even when I'm not aware, proving His...

_____

_____

_____

_____

Day 44

Life and Death

The tongue has the power of life and death,
and those who love it will eat its fruit.

(Proverbs 18:21 NIV)

With our speech, we design and alter our environment. We create new realities. With this ability, we can build up or tear down, edify or discourage, give life or destroy it. The Amplified Bible says: *"Death and life are in the power of the tongue, and those who love it and indulge it will eat its fruit and bear the consequences of their words."*

Jesus, when I say something I regret, please help me to honestly search my heart for the reason. Then I will...

_____

_____

_____

I need a new revelation of the power of my words, Holy Spirit. Help me to speak life, instead of...

_____

_____

_____

Day 44

Reap the Consequences

The tongue can bring death or life;
those who love to talk will reap the consequences.

(Proverbs 18:21 NLT)

The declared word has the capacity to resource earth with Heaven's resources. As believers and reformers we must first pay attention to what we say, realizing that we are actually building the world we have to live in. We have the ability to speak *from* God, revealing His world and His ways. Speaking is not something to be feared—it's a powerful tool, for destruction or creation.

Spending time with God in His Word reveals how and when and why He speaks—from those discoveries I can...

_____

_____

_____

_____

I realize that what I say can either reflect God to the world or deflect Him to...

_____

_____

_____

_____

Day 45

Revealing Our Inheritance

He will glorify and honor Me, because He (the Holy Spirit) will take from what is Mine and will disclose it to you.

(John 16:14 AMP)

In John 16:15, Jesus describes a primary role of the Holy Spirit—revealing to us all that belongs to Him. His inheritance is transferred to our account. Every time God speaks to us, there is a transfer of heavenly resource from His account into ours. Hearing God is essential to release the vastness of our inheritance in Christ. Without the Holy Spirit, it is beyond comprehension.

Holy Spirit, please help me to grasp that fact that Jesus has given me "all things" as an inheritance.

_____

_____

_____

_____

I want to understand more every day what it means for me to be a co-heir with Christ.

_____

_____

_____

_____

Day 45

All Things

All things have been delivered to Me by My Father, and no one knows the Son except the Father. Nor does anyone know the Father except the Son, and the one to whom the Son wills to reveal Him.
(Matthew 11:27 NKJV)

The transfer of "all things," our inheritance, begs this question: "Why would God give us all things?" Answer: Because all things are necessary for us to fulfill the commission that God has given us. Our assignment from God requires the use of "all things" to be under our supervision to accomplish His purposes on earth. Never minimize your call on earth to mere survival. God created you to thrive and to impact the world for His Kingdom.

I will press into my inheritance, pulling on God's supernatural intervention to fulfill my calling so I can...

With the Holy Spirit's guidance, I can release Heaven on earth through...

Day 46

Growing in Favor

*Jesus grew in wisdom and in stature and
in favor with God and all the people.*

(Luke 2:52 NIV)

It's understandable that Jesus would need to increase in favor with people, as it would give Him access and influence within society. But how is it that the Son of God, who is perfect in every way, needs to increase in favor with God? There is no easy answer, but it is clear that if Jesus needed more favor from God to complete His assignment, how much more of an increase do we need!

I want to grow in favor like Jesus did, so I will walk through doors that God opens, even if it feels...

_____

_____

_____

_____

God, please shut every door other than Yours so...

_____

_____

_____

_____

Day 46

Attracting God's Favor

*Jesus grew in wisdom and in stature and in
favor with God and all the people.*

(Luke 2:52 NLT)

As with most everything related to the Kingdom of God, we receive increase through generously giving away what we have. It is no different with favor— grace. Grace is the favor of God—a highly valued heavenly commodity. Grace is significant because it brings transformation through words of encouragement by attracting the favor of God to the person we choose to serve.

God has designed His Kingdom to increase as it is dispersed; therefore, I choose to give grace to _____ and _____ bringing God's favor upon them.

My favor will grow as I share the grace of God, and my life will change significantly because...

_____

_____

_____

_____

Day 47

God's Church

*And I tell you that you are Peter, and on this rock I will build my
church, and the gates of Hades will not overcome it.*

(Matthew 16:18 NIV)

We are first and foremost a people of God's Presence, the eternal dwelling
place of God. Our ministry to God positions and equips us to serve people.
Evangelism in its purest form is simply an overflow of worship. The glory of
God was seen on and within the house(s) of God in the Old Testament—
how much more is that glory witnessed in the house He built, called His
Church.

May I always be known as a worshiper as I...

_____

_____

_____

_____

Help me to never forget, God, that Your dwelling place is in Your Church
and that...

_____

_____

_____

_____

Day 47

Building Upon His Church

*Now I say to you that you are Peter (which means "rock"),
and upon this rock I will build my church, and all the
powers of hell will not conquer it.*

(Matthew 16:18 NLT)

The creative expression of God's Church that comes through His wisdom is a reminder to all that this family of believers is commissioned to bring heavenly answers to earthly problems. Rather than the inferior wisdom of this world, we bring divine wisdom that answers the cry of human hearts.

In light of the Holy Spirit's guidance, I am humble enough yet bold enough to offer help to people who...

_____

_____

_____

I want to use my God-given talents and compassion to help make God's Church famous for love and wisdom by...

_____

_____

_____

God's Manifold Wisdom

Now the manifold wisdom of God might be made known by the church to the principalities and powers in the heavenly places, according to the eternal purpose which He accomplished in Christ Jesus our Lord.

(Ephesians 3:10-11 NKJV)

To resource the earth with Heaven's resources, our understanding of stewardship must grow. Many struggle when leaders teach about our role of stewarding money, which automatically disqualifies them from weightier issues like responsibly managing gifts, time, relationships, and the world we live in. The greatest honor we have is the responsibility to steward tomorrow, today.

I admit to struggling about stewarding money, so I will ask my heavenly Father to work with me on that so I...

_____

_____

_____

_____

Lord, give me Your vision to pull the promises of tomorrow into today and...

_____

_____

_____

_____

Day 48

Shaping the World

God's purpose in all this was to use the church to display his wisdom...
This was his eternal plan, which he carried out
through Christ Jesus our Lord.

(Ephesians 3:10-11 NLT)

Our role in shaping the world around us with God's wisdom is to joyfully learn to pull tomorrow into today. God trains us for this role by awakening and establishing our affections for His Kingdom. His Word comes from eternity into time, giving us a track to ride on and impacting our world through the influence of His world.

God says I have the power to imagine, speak into, and shape the future with Him, so tonight's prayer is...

_____

_____

_____

_____

When settled into God's Presence, I see His Kingdom come and His will be done...

_____

_____

_____

_____

Day 49

Every Purpose and Plan

*Through our union with Christ we too have been claimed by
God as his own inheritance. Before we were even born, he gave
us our destiny; that we would fulfill the plan of God who always
accomplishes every purpose and plan in his heart.*

(Ephesians 1:11 TPT)

The believer's inheritance is beyond human comprehension. He gave us the
gift of His Son's sacrifice, which is beyond comprehension because we have
an assignment beyond reason. Jesus intends to fill the earth with His glory,
and His glorious Church will play a role.

Lord, I want to do all that is in Your heart for me to do, which is...

_____

_____

_____

_____

I know I need to encounter God, renew my mind, and be filled with His...

_____

_____

_____

_____

Day 49

Stewards of Tomorrow

*In Him also we have obtained an inheritance, being predestined
according to the purpose of Him who works all
things according to the counsel of His will.*
(Ephesians 1:11 NKJV)

It's profoundly interesting that we have already inherited tomorrow—things to come—making us stewards of tomorrow. God reveals coming events, and we steward the timing of those events. This amazing privilege is exemplified in Scripture and gives insight to passages that might otherwise be hard to understand.

I trust God that He has a purpose and perfect plan—even when I don't understand because He is...

_____

_____

_____

_____

Leaning into Ephesians 1:11 with the Holy Spirit reveals to me that...

_____

_____

_____

_____

Increase and Acceleration

*"Behold, the days are coming," says the Lord, "when the
plowman shall overtake the reaper, and the treader
of grapes him who sows seed."*
(Amos 9:13 NKJV)

God's Kingdom only knows increase and acceleration. Our hunger accelerates the process of development, growth, and actually speeds up time. I'm convinced that God is ridding us of our excuse concerning "seasons"— blamed for moodiness, unbelief, depression, inactivity, and the like. It must end. As technological development has increased exponentially, so the development and maturity of this generation will increase.

Lord, I want to be part of Your increase, so I am open to Your...

_____

_____

_____

_____

Fill me with the revelation of Your faithfulness, Lord, so I may step into my authority with all boldness and with all...

_____

_____

_____

_____

Day 50

Grain and Grapes

"The time will come," says the Lord, "when the grain and grapes will grow faster than they can be harvested. Then the terraced vineyards on the hills of Israel will drip with sweet wine!"

(Amos 9:13 NLT)

Trees planted by God's river bear fruit 12 months of the year. They are the prophetic prototype of the last days' generation that has experienced the acceleration prophesied. How else do you think it's possible for the plowman to overtake the reaper? This is an amazing prophetic picture of a time when planting and harvesting are done in one motion. There's a message for us in the cursed fig tree. Jesus cursed it for not bearing fruit out of season. He has the right to expect the fruit of the impossible from those He has created for the impossible. The Spirit of the resurrected Christ living in me has disqualified me from the mundane and ordinary. I am qualified for the impossible, because I'm a believing believer.

Nothing that you have done or have failed to accomplish is involved in your qualification to do My works upon the earth.

It's only faith in Me that qualifies you for the impossible.

Day 51

Life's Marathon Race

As for us, we have all of these great witnesses who encircle us like
clouds. ...we will be able to run life's marathon race with passion and
determination, for the path has been already marked out before us.
(Hebrews 12:1 TPT)

We are uniquely positioned with the richest inheritance of all time, accumulated through many centuries of God and human encounters. The righteous dead are watching, filling heavenly stands as the cloud of witnesses. They are invested in us for this final leg of the race, waiting to see what we will do with what we've been given.

Thank You, God, for equipping me to run this race; when I receive the baton I will move...

_____

_____

_____

_____

I come into God's Presence hungry for whatever He has for me today, even if it is...

_____

_____

_____

_____

Day 51

Lay Aside Every Weight

*Therefore we also, since we are surrounded by so great a cloud
of witnesses, let us lay aside every weight, and the sin
which so easily ensnares us, and let us run with
endurance the race that is set before us.*

(Hebrews 12:1 NKJV)

God's language continues to be unveiled, His heart is being imparted, and we have been given the right to surpass the accomplishments of previous generations using His creativity through His wisdom to solve the issues facing us. The witnesses' ceiling is our floor. This is our time to run.

Before I go to sleep I will ask God to show me how I can best pour out His love to people around me. His answer:

_____

_____

_____

_____

The heart of intercession—prayer—is to connect with Him to...

_____

_____

_____

_____

MORNING

Put Away Your Agenda

Believe in me so that rivers of living water will burst out from within you, flowing from your innermost being, just like the Scripture says!
(John 7:38 TPT)

When we go into God's Presence, tapping into the heavenly realm, we are positioned to receive great breakthrough—if we don't have our own agendas. If we already know what we want God to do, we handcuff God for that moment. It's as if we say, "Here God, is my idea; now do it my way." We are no longer partnering with Him.

Father, I want to be a conduit for Your heart on the earth, which means I need to...

_____

_____

_____

_____

Draw me into Your perspective, Lord, and let my prayers birth the dreams of Heaven by...

_____

_____

_____

_____

Day 52

Living Water Flowing from Within

Whoever believes in me, as Scripture has said,
rivers of living water will flow from within them.

(John 7:38 NIV)

I go into His Presence to love Him, to experience "Spirit to spirit." The first time I experienced this, I felt our hearts connecting, as if my heart was beating the same heartbeat as His—pouring upon me "liquid love" from His heart, which was broken for humanity. Our two hearts intertwined as one. When you feel that, when you see His heart broken and His amazing love—your only response can be to pray with burning passion for a lost generation.

Everything God designed is for intimacy with His children; that intimacy looks like...

_____

_____

_____

_____

Prayer with burning passion causes me to...

_____

_____

_____

_____

His Good Promises

Praise be to the Lord, who has given rest to his people Israel
just as he promised. Not one word has failed of all the
good promises he gave through his servant Moses.

(1 Kings 8:56 NIV)

God's yes together with our yes brings about prayer breakthrough. I'm amazed God would choose to partner with us and have us join Him in making history—but after all, we are His children. He is great, all-powerful, and a loving and caring Father who wants to be involved in our lives. He wants us to help build His Kingdom on earth.

Father, what talents and skills do I have that will help me build Your Kingdom:

_____

_____

_____

_____

Partnering with God is the same as...

_____

_____

_____

_____

EVENING

Just as He Promised

Praise the Lord who has given rest to his people Israel, just as he promised. Not one word has failed of all the wonderful promises he gave through his servant Moses.

(1 Kings 8:56 NLT)

I am convinced that God likes my ideas. So when I pray, I pray from a place of security. I go into prayer believing that God is on my side. I feel like our lives can be so intertwined with God's that our thoughts, feelings, and even what we do are melted together with His. When God made us just the way we are, He liked what He made.

I will guard my creativity against voices of criticism by...

_____

_____

_____

_____

May I never crush any of God's ideas because His ideas...

_____

_____

_____

_____

No Longer Infants

Then we will no longer be infants, tossed back and forth by the waves,
and blown here and there by every wind of teaching and by the
cunning and craftiness of people in their deceitful scheming.

(Ephesians 4:14 NIV)

Because we are the offensive team, we pray from victory. If you are not praying as a victor, you will always be trying to protect what God gave you from
the devil's plans, or worse yet, running after the devil to figure out what he's
doing. That's wrong. God gave you the ball—don't pray from fear.

Sometimes I pray from anxiety, overwhelmed by the darkness surrounding
me because I...

_____

_____

_____

_____

Forgive me for losing sight of Your ever-present victory, God, bring me back
to...

_____

_____

_____

_____

Day 54

Not Tossed or Windblown

...We won't be tossed and blown about by every wind of new teaching.
We will not be influenced when people try to trick us
with lies so clever they sound like the truth.

(Ephesians 4:14 NLT)

An offensive team knows where the ball will go, who will catch it, and where to run. They have one focus—get the touchdown. As intercessors, we must listen for the plays the Lord calls, pray them in, catch the ball, and make the touchdown. We are not to worry about the enemy's strategies. We are to make the plays God calls.

Victory is my inheritance—God has rigged the game and I'm thankful...

_____

_____

_____

_____

I know that God's light wins over darkness every time and I am...

_____

_____

_____

_____

Day 55

Confidence in God

You will not be subject to terror, for it will not terrify you.
Nor will the disrespectful be able to push you aside, because
God is your confidence in times of crisis, keeping
your heart at rest in every situation.

(Proverbs 3:25-26 TPT)

Everything is going great in your life and you're walking in peace; then all of a sudden, fear tries to envelop you. We believers must choose to resist fear. The devil has legal rights only if we agree with him. He uses fear to go right for our soft spots. But with our confidence in God, our hearts can rest and peace will return.

I have been afraid many times. Forgive me, Jesus...

_____

_____

_____

_____

Your sacrifice and Your blood is enough, Jesus...

_____

_____

_____

_____

Day 55

Have No Fear

*Have no fear of sudden disaster or of the ruin that
overtakes the wicked, for the Lord will be at your side
and will keep your foot from being snared.*
(Proverbs 3:25-26 NIV)

When I look at the world, I can recognize the devil's simple plan—fear. All the devil has to do is make sure that we walk in fear; then all of our responses will be out of the place of fear. The most repeated command in the Bible is *"Do not fear."* From Genesis to Revelation, God has repeatedly told us not to fear. God knows our humanness.

"DO not fear" is not a suggestion; it is God's command to me; therefore, I will...

_____

_____

_____

_____

God deserves all my trust—which displaces fear and replaces it with...

_____

_____

_____

_____

Day 56

MORNING

Nothing Can Hinder the Lord

*Jonathan said to his young armor-bearer, "Come...Perhaps the Lord
will act in our behalf. Nothing can hinder the Lord
from saving, whether by many or by few."*
(1 Samuel 14:6 NIV)

God wants passionate intercessors with courage. Many or few doesn't matter—it took only one Man who walked this planet over two thousand years
ago to change the world forever. One man! Jesus. Jonathan's attitude is what
we need in our spirits when we are interceding. Numbers have nothing to do
with what God wants to do in the spirit realm. What matters is passion and
courage.

Holy Spirit, infuse me with Jonathan's courage so I can...

_____

_____

_____

_____

I want the faith to know that nothing can hinder the will of God in my...

_____

_____

_____

_____

The Lord Has No Restraints

*Then Jonathan said to the young man who bore his armor, "Come...
it may be that the Lord will work for us. For nothing restrains
the Lord from saving by many or by few."*

(1 Samuel 16:4 NKJV)

Jonathan's passion to see justice bore immediate fruit. The Hebrews and the renegades in hiding, came to Saul's side to fight. The courage of one became the courage of many. Jonathan lived an offensive life. He knew nothing was impossible with God. As we carry out seemingly crazy prophetic acts, choosing to live an offensive life before God, God will fight for us too.

God's Kingdom come is stirring within His creation—I will be a catalyst by...

_____

_____

_____

_____

As a catalyst, I will inspire others to pursue God's Presence with...

_____

_____

_____

_____

MORNING

Reconciled Us to Himself

And God has made all things new, and reconciled us to himself, and given us the ministry of reconciling others to God.

(2 Corinthians 5:18 TPT)

Redding, California, is my home, my land. I believe that what I pray over my city makes a difference. The same is true for where you live is yours. We are spiritual leaders in our land. Several years ago, there was a brutal murder in the city. I wept before God, asking for forgiveness for the murderer, crying for mercy, and praying that God would heal our land from bloodshed.

Forgive me, Father, when I've passed judgment on my city instead of crying out for Your mercy in times of...

_____

_____

_____

_____

Show me what it's like to take true ownership over my land, Lord:

_____

_____

_____

_____

Day 57

Reconciliation and Responsibility

And all of this is a gift from God, who brought us back to himself through Christ. And God has given us this task of reconciling people to him.

(2 Corinthians 5:18 NLT)

As an intercessor, I take ownership over what takes place in my land. You might say, "Wait a minute—you didn't commit the crime, so why are you taking the blame?" Because I have taken spiritual possession over my land and take it personally when something sinful and wrong happens. I see it as my responsibility to make it right through confession and repentance.

I will take hold of the reins over my city, region, and nation for the sake of...

_____

_____

_____

_____

I will declare God's goodness and His heart of mercy to make a difference in...

_____

_____

_____

_____

Day 58

The Happiest People on Earth

We do this by keeping our eyes on Jesus...Because of the joy awaiting him, he endured the cross, disregarding its shame. Now he is seated in the place of honor beside God's throne.

(Hebrews 12:2 NLT)

Intercessors should be the happiest people on the planet because they know God's plans. God is in a good mood and wants to give good gifts to His children. Intercessors are to agree with His plans and bring Heaven to earth. And because Heaven is filled with joy—it's our responsibility to bring that joy to earth.

I want to be as joyful as Jesus was as He spread the Good News of the Kingdom, so I'm going to...

I'll do my best to constantly refresh my mind with God's joy and...

The Joy Set Before Him

...For the joy set before him he endured the cross, scorning its shame, and sat down at the right hand of the throne of God.
(Hebrews 12:2 NIV)

Jesus endured so much while on earth—for the promise of joy that was set before Him. Jesus is into joy! God's Son endured being human, for Heaven's joy. He endured the suffering of being in a human body after living in the heavenly realm full of light, power, and joy! In my opinion, the joy is what sustained Him while living on earth and dying on a cross.

From now on, the joy of Heaven will be my motivation and my...

_____

_____

_____

_____

God's promise of a joyful reward encourages me and...

_____

_____

_____

_____

Day 59

Oil of Joy

You have loved righteousness and hated wickedness; therefore
God, your God, has set you above your companions
by anointing you with the oil of joy.

(Hebrews 1:9 NIV)

In this Scripture verse, God is speaking about His Son, Jesus. Because He loved righteousness and hated lawlessness, God gave Him the oil of joy, or gladness. Joy is one of Heaven's greatest treasures. God anointed Jesus with gladness, which means exuberant joy. Jesus is our example; therefore we should carry that same anointing. An anointing of exuberant joy was poured over Jesus. May it be so for us!

Jesus, please anoint me with a new revelation of Your joy; I accept it with...

_____

_____

_____

_____

Help me, Jesus, value joy the way You did while here on earth so I can...

_____

_____

_____

_____

Day 59

EVENING

Hanging with Jesus

You have loved righteousness and hated lawlessness;
therefore God, Your God, has anointed You with the oil of
gladness more than Your companions.
(Hebrews 1:9 NKJV)

When we hang around in the Presence of Jesus, we will connect with Heaven's joy. As the long-wedded couple resembles each other, the more we spend time with Jesus, the more we will become like Him. You want more joy? Do what the psalmist did in Psalm 73. He went before God, poured out his heart, and he found God's Presence. God will gladly trade His joy for our worries.

God's heart is that I would perpetually live in the life-giving strength of His joy. I aim to please God, so I...

_____

_____

_____

_____

God's arms are always open wide to welcome me when I...

_____

_____

_____

_____

Day 60

God's Every Word

But He answered and said, "It is written, 'Man shall not live by bread alone, but by every word that proceeds from the mouth of God.'"
(Matthew 4:4 NKJV)

When the devil says, "If you are the son of God, command this stone to become bread," he was trying to get Jesus to fight on his terms (see Matthew 4:3). Jesus could've easily turned stone into bread. But Jesus wouldn't enter this realm of thinking; He didn't even address the identity part of the question. Jesus knew who He was and pulled His answer directly from God's Word.

I pray to always get my answers directly from God's Word, assuring...

_____

_____

_____

_____

I'm holding out to You today the problem weighing on my heart, Lord. Please give me a word...

_____

_____

_____

_____

Every Word of God

But Jesus told him, "No! The Scriptures say, 'People do not live by bread alone, but by every word that comes from the mouth of God.'"
(Matthew 4:4 NLT)

The devil is more than happy to let us in on his schemes and strategies if it distracts us from what Heaven is doing. Jesus was the ultimate Intercessor, and He saw right though the devil's tricks. The devil was looking for just a little agreement. But Jesus was in complete control of the conversation. He never once gave the devil fuel for his madness.

The spiritual playing ground is not level with competing sides—He has already won! Being on the winning side feels...

_____

_____

_____

_____

When I stay connected to God, we can together watch victories unfold...

_____

_____

_____

_____

A Joyful Shout!

Make a joyful shout to the Lord, all you lands! Serve the Lord with gladness; come before His presence with singing. Know that the Lord, He is God; it is He who has made us, and not we ourselves; we are His people and the sheep of His pasture.

(Psalm 100:1-3 NKJV)

Worship is a feeling or attitude within that keeps us close to God. It's not just attending church on Sunday and singing songs during the worship service. Even though that is important, it's not the most important. Worship comes from within us and goes with us throughout our days.

God, I joyfully shout to You because of who...

_____

_____

_____

_____

Some have memorized Psalm 100 as children. I have/have not memorized Scripture because...

_____

_____

_____

_____

Day 61

Worship with Gladness!

*Shout for joy to the Lord, all the earth. Worship the Lord with
gladness; come before him with joyful songs. Know that the
Lord is God. It is he who made us, and we are his;
we are his people, the sheep of his pasture.*

(Psalm 100:1-3 NIV)

When we are focused on God, His power and Presence enter into our worship. One Sunday morning, I heard Holy Spirit whisper, "You are being distracted from Me; just worship Me." I realized that I needed to be centered on God and worshiping Him. He would take care of any spiritual matters in the room. My spiritual warfare weapon was to worship Him.

Warfare is not difficult or complicated; set your gaze on God and He will handle...

_____

_____

_____

_____

Focusing on God and letting everything else fade away is harder when I...

_____

_____

_____

_____

Day 62

God's Presence

*The Lord replied, "My Presence will go
with you, and I will give you rest."*
(Exodus 33:14 NIV)

How do you want people to remember you? People work so hard to create
an image and form a reputation for themselves. For some it's their beauty or
skills or place in society. Others work hard to create an image from their spiritual gifts. The Bible even teaches us the value of a good name (see Proverbs
22:1). It is obviously important, if done correctly.

If I could choose one thing to be known for, one thing that would distin-
guish me from everyone else, it would be...

_____

_____

_____

_____

What truly matters is to be known as a person who carries God's Presence,
meaning...

_____

_____

_____

_____

Day 62

Everything Will Be Fine

*The Lord replied, "I will personally go with you, Moses,
and I will give you rest—everything will be fine for you."*
(Exodus 33:14 NLT)

God chose Israel's reputation for them. At least He chose what He wanted it to be. They were the least of all, the most insignificant of all, the weakest of all nations. There was nothing about their natural qualities that made them stand out from any other people group. But one thing set them apart—the glory of God—His manifested Presence would be their distinguishing mark.

Knowing God personally goes with me, I'm confident that everything will be...

When I join myself to God, He will bring me into the land of His promise where I am free to...

Righteousness, Peace, Joy

For the kingdom of God is not a matter of eating and drinking,
but of righteousness, peace and joy in the Holy Spirit.

(Romans 14:17 NIV)

Jesus taught, *"Seek first the kingdom of God and His righteousness, and all these things shall be added to you"* (Matthew 6:33 NKJV). The Kingdom of God is not separate from His actual Presence. In reality, the Kingdom of God is within the Presence of the Spirit of God. *"For the kingdom of God is...in the Holy Spirit"* (Romans 14:17). This command by Jesus directs us to prioritize our lives resulting in righteous living.

Righteous living to me means...

_____

_____

_____

_____

How exciting to be invited into a Kingdom built on Your Presence, God! Thank You for...

_____

_____

_____

_____

Day 63

A Life of Goodness

For the Kingdom of God is not a matter of what we eat or drink, but of living a life of goodness and peace and joy in the Holy Spirit.
(Romans 14:17 NLT)

When we discuss our responsibilities in life, many good things come to our minds. But for me now it always boils down to His Presence. What do I do with His Presence? What place does the manifest Presence of God have with how I think and live? Does the Presence of God affect the vision and focus of my life? What is the impact of His Presence on my behavior?

Goodness, peace, and joy in the Holy Spirit brings to mind pure...

_____

_____

_____

_____

There is no higher calling for me other than...

_____

_____

_____

_____

Day 64

A Sound from Heaven

And suddenly there came a sound from heaven, as of a rushing
mighty wind, and it filled the whole house where they were sitting.
(Acts 2:2 NKJV)

The sound during the disciples' prayer meeting after Jesus' death carried a reality from that world into this one. This heavenly sound transformed the atmosphere over the city of Jerusalem. In one moment, Jerusalem was changed from the city that crucified Jesus to a city that wanted to know how to be saved. How did that happen? Through *"a sound from Heaven."*

Holy Spirit, open my ears to hear the sounds of Heaven that will...

_____

_____

_____

_____

I want to be surrounded with sounds from Heaven that shake my world...

_____

_____

_____

_____

Day 64

The Roar Filled the House

Suddenly, there was a sound from heaven like the roaring of a mighty windstorm, and it filled the house where they were sitting.

(Acts 2:2 NLT)

The house of God is the gate of Heaven—built on the edge of two worlds. The heavenly sound was heard and experienced on earth. The roar of Heaven summoned the city to its purpose and call. In this moment, two worlds collided, and the inferior realm of darkness gave way to the superior nature of His Kingdom. We have the unique privilege of carrying His Presence, which causes conflict so that the two realities—Heaven and earth—can dance together in perfect harmony.

My light will always chase away darkness.

_____

_____

_____

_____

I long to release this light through you to the world!

_____

_____

_____

_____

God's Spirit Poured Out

I will no longer hide my face from them, for I will pour out my
Spirit on the people of Israel, declares the Sovereign Lord.
(Ezekiel 39:29 NIV)

Many assume the baptism in the Holy Spirit is primarily to make us more useful in ministry. Instead, this unimaginable privilege of carrying His Presence should never reduce us to a mere laborer for God. While it is one of my highest privileges to serve Him completely, my labor is the byproduct of my love for Him. This baptism introduces us to intimacy at the highest possible level.

I love You, Jesus, and the depths...

Thank You, Jesus, for coming to turn the world upside down by sacrificing Your life so I could live in union with God forever, and...

Never Again

*I will never again turn my face from them, for I will pour out my
Spirit upon the people of Israel. I, the Sovereign Lord, have spoken!*
(Ezekiel 39:29 NLT)

In the outpouring of the Holy Spirit is the revelation of God's face. There
is nothing greater. Ezekiel 39:29 links God's face and His favor with the
outpouring of His Spirit, which is available for everyone. The outpouring in
Acts 2 was the beginning and the fulfillment of the quest for God's face and
Presence.

There is nothing more worthy of my life's devotion than...

_____

_____

_____

_____

To receive God's love, pursue His Spirit, and host His Presence is my prayer
this evening...

_____

_____

_____

_____

Dancing Before the Lord

*David retorted to Michal, "I was dancing before the Lord, who chose
me above your father and all his family! ...So I celebrate before
the Lord. Yes, and I am willing to look even more foolish
than this, even to be humiliated in my own eyes!"*

(2 Samuel 6:21-22 NLT)

When the Ark was returned to Jerusalem, King David stripped himself of
his kingly garments and put on basically a priest's undergarment and danced
in an undignified fashion. He is known as the man after God's heart—God's
Presence. It might surprise us to discover just what God finds glorifying.

I pray I will dance before the Lord unashamedly like David...

_____

_____

_____

_____

I want more of Your Presence at any cost, God, including my...

_____

_____

_____

_____

Day 66

EVENING

Humiliated and Honored

*I will become even more undignified than this, and I will be
humiliated in my own eyes. But by these slave girls
you spoke of, I will be held in honor.*

(2 Samuel 6:22 NIV)

David's wife Michal was appalled at his complete lack of public decorum.
Instead of greeting him with honor, she tried to shame him. Her disregard
for the Presence of God reveals the same lack of value for God's Presence as
her father Saul during his reign. David clearly states in verse 22 his intent to
become even more embarrassing in her eyes, because He prized God's favor.

God delights when I worship Him—which I do as often as...

_____

_____

_____

_____

God's heart is moved when believers like David fully praise and worship
Him; I will likewise...

_____

_____

_____

_____

Day 67

Like a Dove

*Then, as John baptized Jesus he spoke these words: "I see the Spirit of
God appear like a dove descending from the heavenly
realm and landing upon him—and it rested
upon him from that moment forward!"*
(John 1:32 TPT)

Jesus sets the stage for a whole new spiritual experience. The Old Testament
prophets modeled the possibility of living with God's Presence amazingly,
especially for their day. They showed the impact of the Presence of God
upon a person for a specific task. But Jesus revealed this as a lifestyle. The
Holy Spirit rested upon Him from then on.

Thank You, Father, that everyone can be blessed with receiving Your Holy
Spirit for...

_____

_____

_____

_____

Your Spirit empowers me to follow Jesus' model of living in intimacy with
You...

_____

_____

_____

_____

The Spirit Remained

And John bore witness, saying, "I saw the Spirit descending from heaven like a dove, and He remained upon Him."

(John 1:32 NKJV)

I realize we are not to live by feelings. Emotions are wonderful, but not reliable indicators of God's Presence. But there is a feeling that goes beyond emotions, and quite frankly can work regardless of our emotional state. It is the mood of the Holy Spirit Himself that we can become so in tune with that we move as He moves. It's like a dance when God and I move together to impact the world.

When Spirit filled, I'm always in sync with God's gentle guidance, moving...

_____

_____

_____

I would describe the "mood of the Holy Spirit" as...

_____

_____

_____

Holy Spirit Power

But you shall receive power when the Holy Spirit has come upon you;
and you shall be witnesses to Me in Jerusalem, and in all Judea and
Samaria, and to the end of the earth.

(Acts 1:8 NKJV)

The Holy Spirit lives in born-again believers and He will never leave us. What a promise and comfort! But the sad reality is that the Holy Spirit doesn't rest upon every believer. He is in us for our sake, but He is upon us for the sake of others. When the Holy Spirit rests without withdrawing, it is because He has had an honorable welcome.

Holy Spirit, please rest upon me like You did Jesus, so I can...

_____

_____

_____

_____

When Your tangible Presence is in my life, I have the power to...

_____

_____

_____

_____

Day 68

Holy Spirit Grief

And do not grieve the Holy Spirit of God.
(Ephesians 4:30 NKJV)

Do not quench the Spirit.
(1 Thessalonians 5:19 NKJV)

To not grieve the Holy Spirit is a command focused on the issue of sin—in thought, attitude, or action. Grieve means to cause sorrow or distress and describes the pain the heart of the Holy Spirit can feel because of something we would do or allow in our lives. It is character centered—and a vital boundary for anyone focused on hosting His Presence more powerfully.

Holy Spirit, is there any part of my life—anything that I have grown accustomed to—that grieves You? Please, bring it to mind now so I can...

_____

_____

_____

_____

Lord, I never want to grieve You; help me to...

_____

_____

_____

_____

Peace Upon This House

Once you enter a house, speak to the people there and say, "God's blessing of peace be upon this house!" If a lover of peace resides there, your peace will rest upon that household. But if you are rejected, your blessing of peace will come back upon you.

(Luke 10:5-6 TPT)

The world thinks peace is the absence of—war, noise, conflict, etc. For believers, Peace is a Person—Jesus. Our response to Jesus' command to release peace over a household is directly tied to our recognizing the Presence of the Holy Spirit. Consciousness of His Presence always increases our impact to influence the world around us.

You are my King and my Lord and I am ready to…

_____

_____

_____

_____

Lord, increase my awareness of Your Presence so the Prince of Peace can…

_____

_____

_____

_____

EVENING

Prince of Peace

When you enter a house, first say, "Peace to this house."
If someone who promotes peace is there, your peace will
rest on them; if not, it will return to you.

(Luke 10:5-6 NIV)

Jesus is the Prince of Peace. The Holy Spirit is the Spirit of Christ, the Person of Peace, who is the actual atmosphere of Heaven. Peace is calming and wonderful for the believer, but highly destructive for the powers of darkness. Believers are to release the Person of Peace when entering a home, releasing the Presence to yielded hearts and undermining the powers of darkness. For Jesus, this was Ministry 101.

Learning to release God's peace means that I need to...

_____

_____

_____

_____

Being filled with the peace and Presence of Heaven is...

_____

_____

_____

_____

Preparation

*So above all, constantly chase after the realm of God's kingdom
and the righteousness that proceeds from him. Then all these less
important things will be given to you abundantly.*

(Matthew 6:33 TPT)

If I was sending out the disciples (Matthew 28:18-20), I would've taken care
of all the contacts, meeting places, finances, and sufficient training. I would
have also sent people to each city beforehand to prepare the way. I am constantly amazed at how differently Jesus thinks from how I think. He sent
them on a journey that He knew was fully prepared—because God would
be with them.

Thank You, Jesus, for preparing me for the journey I am facing right now to...

_____

_____

_____

_____

I am prepared because You will be with me, and You don't miss...

_____

_____

_____

_____

Day 70

Provision

But seek first his kingdom and his righteousness,
and all these things will be given to you as well.

(Matthew 6:33 NIV)

Jesus provided the disciples direction and the Presence in the power and authority given to them. He ensured natural provisions through the Holy Spirit at work. His Kingdom works entirely on the "first things first" principle. The Lord's supernatural provision is divine protection and fully impacts our assignment. The whole issue is to give up the reins of being in control to becoming truly Holy-Spirit empowered and directed.

God, I know you cared about where the disciples would sleep and eat. You were teaching them that if they focused on Your Presence, what they needed would...

_____

_____

_____

As I focus on You, what I need will...

_____

_____

_____

Day 71

God's Wrap-Around Presence

Because you are close to me and always available,
my confidence will never be shaken, for I experience your
wrap-around presence every moment.
(Psalm 16:8 TPT)

In Heaven there are no thoughts void of God. He is the Light, Life, and Heart of His spiritual realm. Heaven is filled with perfect confidence and trust in God. On the other hand, this earthly realm is filled with mistrust and chaos. We will always release the reality of the realm we are most aware of. Living aware of God is an essential part of the command to abide in Him.

"Living aware of God" means that I must change the way I...

_____

_____

_____

_____

God's wrap-around Presence would feel to me like He is...

_____

_____

_____

_____

Right Beside Me

I know the Lord is always with me.
I will not be shaken, for he is right beside me.
(Psalm 16:8 NLT)

Living with a continual awareness of Him is a supreme goal for anyone who understands the privilege of hosting His Presence. He is the *Holy* Spirit, making holiness a huge focus of our lives. Yet I get concerned when people have the holiness ambition without acknowledging first the cornerstone of Christian theology—God is good. A holy lifestyle is the natural result of delighting in the Lord, who accepts us as we are.

I welcome the Holy Spirit to work His way within me and...

_____

_____

_____

_____

I can feel God smiling at me sometimes and it fills me with...

_____

_____

_____

_____

The Living God

My soul longs, yes, even faints for the courts of the Lord;
my heart and my flesh cry out for the living God.
(Psalm 84:2 NKJV)

I'm not sure when it happened, or even how it happened, but somewhere in church history the focus of our corporate gatherings became the sermon. Not to devalue the Scriptures, it's just that the physical presence of a Bible should never become the replacement for the Spirit of God upon His people. Somehow, we must rediscover the practical nature of the Presence of God being central to all we do and are.

I never want to lose sight of Your Presence as my number-one priority, God. Teach me to...

_____

_____

_____

_____

I will camp myself around Your Presence for the rest of my life...

_____

_____

_____

_____

Day 72

Fainting, Longing, Shouting

I long, yes, I faint with longing to enter the courts of the Lord. With my whole being, body and soul, I will shout joyfully to the living God.
(Psalm 84:2 NLT)

It's been said of the early Church that 95 percent of their activities would have stopped had the Holy Spirit been removed. It's also stated that 95 percent of the modernChurch's activities will continue as normal because there is so little recognition of His Presence. Thankfully, these percentages are changing, as God has been retooling us for His last-days thrust of Presence and harvest.

God loves His Church, but the rituals of gathering on Sunday mean nothing apart from His Presence...

_____

_____

_____

My church's emphasis on the Holy Spirit is...

_____

_____

_____

The Practicality of Presence

*Trust in and rely confidently on the Lord with all your heart
and do not rely on your own insight or understanding.*
(Proverbs 3:5 AMP)

A truly arrogant thought is that the Presence of God isn't practical. Such a lie keeps believers from discovering His nearness. Living conscious of His Presence with us is one of the most essential parts to our earthly life. His name is Emmanuel—God with us. We inherited the God-with-us lifestyle from Jesus. We must live it with the same priority of Presence to have the same impact and purpose as He did.

Thank You, God, that there is not one area of my life that You overlook...

_____

_____

_____

_____

I can go to God like a child, sharing every part of my heart, even...

_____

_____

_____

_____

Day 73
EVENING

Trust in the Lord

Trust in the Lord with all your heart,
and lean not on your own understanding.
(Proverbs 3:5 NKJV)

Trust takes us beyond understanding into realms that only faith can discover. Trust is built on interaction and the resulting discovery of His nature, which is good and perfect in every way. We don't believe because we understand. We understand because we believe. To acknowledge Him is the natural result when we trust Him. The One we trust above our own existence is to be recognized in every aspect and part of life.

I want to have a revelation of God's nature in every area of my life; making it so will require...

_____

_____

_____

_____

God tells me to set my eyes on Him and place my hope in His hands; yes, I...

_____

_____

_____

_____

Day 74

Pray Passionately

Pray passionately in the Spirit, as you constantly intercede with
every form of prayer at all times. Pray the blessings
of God upon all his believers.

(Ephesians 6:18 TPT)

The Presence of God is discovered in prayer. And while that is an obvious truth, many people learn to pray without the Presence, thinking their discipline is what God is looking for. Discipline is important in walking with Christ, for sure. But Christianity is not to be known for disciplines—rather for passions. Prayer is the ultimate expression of partnership with God.

I can pray with Your heart and from Your perspective when I first...

_____

_____

_____

_____

Thank You for the ways I have grown in discipline, but let it never overshadow my adoration of You...

_____

_____

_____

_____

Day 74

Praying Always

Praying always with all prayer and supplication in the Spirit,
being watchful to this end with all perseverance
and supplication for all the saints.
(Ephesians 6:18 NKJV)

When we pray anointed prayers, we are praying the heart of God. His heart is expressed through words, emotion, and decree. Finding the heart of God unlocks His Presence. When praying in tongues, the Presence of God washes over us to bring great refreshing. It's a bit sad when people emphasize that tongues is the least of the gifts. Every gift from God is wonderful, glorious, and extremely necessary to live in His full intentions for us.

I have/have not received the gift of tongues...

_____

_____

_____

_____

I welcome every gift God wants to give me...

_____

_____

_____

_____

Works Prepared Beforehand

For we are His workmanship, created in Christ Jesus for good works,
which God prepared beforehand that we should walk in them.
(Ephesians 2:10 NKJV)

During my prayer times, I carry paper and pen with me because I often get ideas while I'm praying. I used to think it was the devil distracting me. But now I realize that time in His Presence releases creative thoughts such as projects long forgotten, activities for my family, people to call. Ideas flow freely in this environment because that's the way He is. I get ideas in the Presence I wouldn't get anywhere else.

Jesus has the best ideas, solutions, and strategies for every area of my life, including...

_____

_____

_____

_____

Nothing slips past God's attention, and I'm so thankful because...

_____

_____

_____

_____

EVENING

Created in Christ Jesus

For we are God's handiwork, created in Christ Jesus to do good
works, which God prepared in advance for us to do.

(Ephesians 2:10 NIV)

When we realize prayer time "interruptions" are from God interacting with us, we can enjoy the process much more and give Him thanks for having concern for us. If it matters to you, it matters to Him. To keep from leaving the privilege of prayerfully interacting with God to work on other things, I write down what comes to mind so I can return to worshiping and fellowshipping with Him.

I am ready walk in the good works God prepared for me such as...

_____

_____

_____

_____

I never really realized that what matters to me also matters to God...

_____

_____

_____

_____

The Ultimate Pleasure

Neither height nor depth, nor anything else in all creation,
will be able to separate us from the love of God
that is in Christ Jesus our Lord.

(Romans 8:39 NIV)

Turning my attention toward God's love for me actually increases my love for Him. His love is the ultimate pleasure and must be treasured. Many have been raised thinking prayer is a lot of work. Actually, I still value that model, but now only when it comes out of a Presence lifestyle. Discovering His Presence daily is the surest way to stay in love.

I can feast on God's love every minute of every day...

_____

_____

_____

_____

God's love drives out all fear, allowing me to focus on His...

_____

_____

_____

_____

Due North

*But each day the Lord pours his unfailing love upon me, and through
each night I sing his songs, praying to God who gives me life.*
(Psalm 42:8 NLT)

Psalmist David made it a daily practice to place God right in front of him—
this was how he did life. Considering the outcome of David's life, it's not a
stretch to say God's Presence was a secret to David's success. He knew that
if he didn't turn his attention toward the Lord, he would lack the due north
reference point that puts in place everything in life.

Psalm 42:8 speaks to me; my personal paraphrase of the verse is...

_____

_____

_____

_____

I yearn for a life saturated with God's love, intricately intertwined with His
Presence, and...

_____

_____

_____

_____

Life-Changing Encounters

Then Moses said, "I will now turn aside and see this great sight, why the bush does not burn." So when the Lord saw that he turned aside to look, God called to him from the midst of the bush and said, "Moses, Moses!" And he said, "Here I am."

(Exodus 3:3-4 NKJV)

God has had many interesting encounters with His people. It's a mistake to use one as the standard for all. The two most life-changing encounters I've had with God are very different. The first was when I was electrocuted in His Presence for hours. The other one was so subtle it could have been easily missed.

Show up any way You want, Holy Spirit...

_____

_____

_____

_____

Subtle or dramatic, I welcome You to...

_____

_____

_____

_____

Day 77

Wind, Earthquake, Fire

*...but the Lord was not in the wind; and after the wind an
earthquake, but the Lord was not in the earthquake; and after the
earthquake a fire, but the Lord was not in the fire;
and after the fire a still small voice.*

(1 Kings 19:11-12 NKJV)

It's not how extreme an encounter is with God—it's how much of His Presence He can entrust to us. Jesus manifested an intensely practical lifestyle while on earth. Likewise, we can carry the Presence of the Holy Spirit and reveal God to this dying world. Jesus had this in mind when He commissioned His disciples—and us (John 20:21).

I follow Jesus' lead by...

_____

_____

_____

_____

I am listening carefully for the Lord's still small voice...

_____

_____

_____

Day 78

A Steadfast Mind

You will keep in perfect and constant peace the one whose mind is steadfast [that is, committed and focused on You—in both inclination and character], because he trusts and takes refuge in You [with hope and confident expectation].

(Isaiah 26:3 AMP)

Some seasons of life are full of diverse activities, others are less busy. While intense focus restricts us somewhat, it also opens our eyes to see what we hunger for. Self-control is not the ability to say no to a thousand other voices. It's the ability to say yes to the One so completely that all other options fall into the perfect priority.

The season I'm in right now seems to be...

_____

_____

_____

_____

Is this a season to pare down what's competing for my attention?

_____

_____

_____

The Measure of Presence

You will keep him in perfect peace, whose mind
is stayed on You, because he trusts in You.
(Isaiah 26:3 NKJV)

The Holy Spirit is our greatest gift and must become our single focus. God targets each of us for a specific encounter that will redefine our purpose on planet earth. We must have frequent encounters with God that continuously recalibrate our hearts that we may be entrusted with more and more of God. God will give us the measure of His Presence that we are willing to jealously guard.

I won't settle for a life less than what God has promised me, meaning...

_____

_____

_____

_____

Pursuing God's Presence with a fierce focus will bring encounters that...

_____

_____

_____

_____

The New Covenant

After supper he [Jesus] took another cup of wine and said, "This cup is the new covenant between God and his people—an agreement confirmed with my blood, which is poured out as a sacrifice for you.

(Luke 22:20 NLT)

After Jesus' blood was spilled for the New Covenant, we became not only heirs of Abraham, but also co-heirs with Christ's inheritance. What Jesus did for all humanity on the Cross was unconditional. He will never go back or change His mind. Accessing the fullness of the blessing of this covenant, though, is our choice entirely.

I want to receive every part of the inheritance You paid for, Jesus, and use it for Your glory and...

_____

_____

_____

_____

I won't let any aspect of Your covenant with me go unexplored, including...

_____

_____

_____

_____

His Blood Poured Out

*In the same way, after the supper he took the cup, saying, "This cup is
the new covenant in my blood, which is poured out for you."*
(Luke 22:20 NIV)

Taking Communion reminds us of Jesus' sacrifice and the personal, unprecedented ways this New Covenant affects every area of our lives. His blood shed was a covenant promise for all eternity. Jesus paid for everything; His blood washed us white as snow to provide access to the Lord's Presence without an intermediary and without fear. Hell is defeated. We have freedom and authority to boldly release Heaven on earth.

I can run into God's arms without fear or hesitation right now...

_____

_____

_____

_____

Jesus gave His life so I can...

_____

_____

_____

_____

Day 80

Pain and Suffering

Surely he took up our pain and bore our suffering...the
punishment that brought us peace was on him,
and by his wounds we are healed.

(Isaiah 3:5 NIV)

Jesus died for our sins and for our sicknesses. When He went to the Cross, He carried with Him every dark thing of the enemy—Jesus was the eternal sacrifice on our behalf. This passage in Isaiah 53 prophesies the crucifixion and the only moment God ever turned His face from Jesus. When Jesus took the weight of sin upon Himself, God could not be part of that.

Thank You for taking on the isolating burden of my sin so that I could live forever...

_____

_____

_____

_____

For Jesus to be without His Father's Presence even for a moment must have been...

_____

_____

_____

_____

Griefs and Sorrows

Surely He has borne our griefs and carried our sorrows...the
chastisement for our peace was upon Him,
and by His stripes we are healed.

(Isaiah 53:4-5 NKJV)

Isaiah 53:3 describes Jesus' rejection by humanity, saying He was *"a Man of sorrows and acquainted with grief."* That word *grief* is the Hebrew word *choliy*, meaning "sickness, disease, or sadness"—from a root word that means "to be worn down." Jesus carried all of our sorrows, anxieties, and illnesses to the Cross and died so we could be *sozo*—healed in spirit, soul, and body.

Jesus came to offer people an exchange—our burdens for His freedom, our sickness for His strength, our sorrow for His joy. How can I ever repay Him...

_____

_____

_____

_____

The depth of my gratitude is...

_____

_____

_____

_____

A Living Faith

*In this way, every generation will have a living faith in the laws
of life and will never forget the faithful ways of God.*
(Psalm 78:7 TPT)

This verse in Psalm 78 draws the connection between memory, trust, and obedience. Dwelling on the goodness of God, continually reminding ourselves of His faithfulness and His promises—these are the building blocks of trust. And when we trust God, aligning ourselves with His commandments comes so much more naturally. Without keeping Him in the forefront of our minds, that confidence crumbles, and fear takes hold.

I want to be forever building my trust in You, God, to better...

_____

_____

_____

_____

Dear Lord, help me see Your hand in my life in a way that keeps me aware of Your...

_____

_____

_____

_____

Day 81

Never Forget

*Then they would put their trust in God and would not forget
his deeds but would keep his commands.*
(Psalm 78:7 NIV)

There are very real consequences to forgetting who God is. When His goodness and faithfulness are not fresh in our mind, we can become calloused toward Him—leading to an ungrateful heart. We can see the results of that within our own lives and the lives of the Israelites. We live under the New Covenant, and God promised never to remove His Presence from us. It is our choice.

God asks, "Will you trust in My love for you? Will you remember when I have smiled upon your life?" My answer...

_____

_____

_____

_____

I will turn away from fear and self-reliance and choose to be dependent on God's love...

_____

_____

_____

_____

A Sacrifice of Praise

He who offers a sacrifice of praise and thanksgiving honors Me;
and to him who orders his way rightly [who follows the way
that I show him], I shall show the salvation of God.

(Psalm 50:23 AMP)

First Peter 2:9 says that we have been made *"a royal priesthood."* As believers under the New Covenant, we now have the privilege of ministering to the Lord as priests. When we offer up a *"sacrifice of praise,"* we bring honor to God. Focusing our hearts on gratitude brings Him glory, which alone is enough.

I want my every breath to bring You glory, Father. May my praise bring joy to Your heart and...

If I am avoiding the "sacrifice of praise," I invite Your Holy Spirit to show me right now...

Day 82

A Sacrifice of Gratitude

But giving thanks is a sacrifice that truly honors me.
If you keep to my path, I will reveal to you the salvation of God.

(Psalm 50:23 NLT)

The Bible explains that gratitude reorients us correctly, inviting the *"salvation of God"* into our lives. That word *salvation* in Hebrew means "rescue and safety"; it also means "deliverance, prosperity, and victory." The psalmist says to *"enter into His gates with thanksgiving, and into His courts with praise"* (Psalm 100:4 NKJV). When approaching the Lord with thankfulness, we access His Presence and His covering. We can participate in His victory.

The fullness of His Presence is attracted by my praise. Therefore I will...

_____

_____

_____

_____

The fragrance of my gratitude, acknowledges His goodness and draws me into His inner sanctuary where...

_____

_____

_____

_____

Day 83

Christ Lives In Me

My old self has been crucified with Christ.
It is no longer I who live, but Christ lives in me....
(Galatians 2:20 NLT)

We need to remember the greater reality. It's as if God says, "Listen, I know some days are hard and the reality of Heaven seems far away. Maybe your child is sick, or you lost your job, or you did what you swore you would stop doing. I know. I left you My body and My blood to remind you who you are and where your true home is. Remember My salvation, My healing, My Presence, and My victorious return."

You are the compass of my life, Father...

_____

_____

_____

_____

Help me to be everything You created me to be so that the world...

_____

_____

_____

_____

EVENING

Crucified with Christ

I have been crucified with Christ [that is, in Him I have shared His crucifixion]; it is no longer I who live, but Christ lives in me....

(Galatians 2:20 AMP)

Communion is about lining up with Christ—spirit, soul, and body. A time to remember the debt of sin that hung around our necks—too big for us to ever repay—and the way Jesus took that debt with Him to the Cross so we could have abundant life (see John 10:10). It's an opportunity to come into the Presence of the Lord to praise and celebrate with other believers.

In remembrance, I will align with Heaven's perspective of who I am in Christ...

_____

_____

_____

_____

Because of Jesus' sacrifice, I'm protected, loved, provided for, a source of...

_____

_____

_____

_____

Saved and Being Saved

*My beloved ones, just like you've always listened to everything I've
taught you in the past, I'm asking you now to keep following my
instructions...you must continue to make this new life
fully manifested as you live in the holy awe of God—
which brings you trembling into his presence.*

(Philippians 2:12 TPT)

Communion declares that Jesus died for us and is returning for us. When
we surrender our life to Jesus, we are born again—saved. The implication in
Philippians 2:12 is that we are also *being* saved. This doesn't deny what happened when we received Christ. It just emphasizes the daily ongoing process
of personal transformation.

I welcome being transformed by God's gentle guidance to...

_____

_____

_____

_____

Becoming more like Jesus every day is...

_____

_____

_____

_____

Complete Salvation

*Therefore, my dear friends, as you have always obeyed—not only in
my presence, but now much more in my absence—continue to work
out your salvation with fear and trembling.*

(Philippians 2:12 NIV)

Not only were you once saved, but you are to *"continue to work out your salvation."* The glorious truth of salvation comes when we die to meet Him or He returns to take us to Heaven—then our salvation will be complete. Communion is a wonderful privilege that addresses the past and future. Sharing in the broken body and the shed blood of Jesus helps us with the present.

Living within the tension of "now" and "not yet" is part of the divine wrestle of human life, which…

_____

_____

_____

_____

I will take my questions to God and…

_____

_____

_____

_____

Blessed Are the Poor in Spirit

Blessed are the poor in spirit, for theirs is the kingdom of heaven.
(Matthew 5:3 NIV)

How would you describe a group of people who left cities for days at a time, traveling great distances on foot, abandoning all that life involves, only to follow Jesus to some desolate place? Those who had just watched Jesus perform the miraculous, pulled a reality from the heart of God that they didn't even know existed. I call them "poor in spirit." The actual Presence of the Spirit of God upon Jesus stirred up a hunger for God in the people and created a new perspective in them.

Keep me poor in spirit, God. I want every encounter with You to stir up...

_____

_____

_____

_____

Poor in spirit means to me...

_____

_____

_____

_____

Day 85

Theirs Is the Kingdom

*Blessed [spiritually prosperous, happy, to be admired] are the poor
in spirit [those devoid of spiritual arrogance, those who regard
themselves as insignificant], for theirs is the kingdom
of heaven [both now and forever].*

(Matthew 5:3 AMP)

The Sermon on the Mount is a treatise on the Kingdom. In it, Jesus reveals
the attitudes that help His followers access His unseen world. The Kingdom comes in the Presence of the Spirit of God. The crowd recognized and
longed for His Presence. Hunger for God brings about the ultimate humility.
The Beatitudes (see Matthew 5:3-12) Jesus taught are actually the "lenses"
through which the Kingdom is seen.

Lord, may Your Presence shape the way I think about...

_____

_____

_____

_____

Blessings and joy will be the fruit of our relationship when I...

_____

_____

_____

_____

Sincere and Adoring Worshipers

From here on, worshiping the Father will not be a matter of the right place but with the right heart. For God is a Spirit, and he longs to have sincere worshipers who worship and adore him in the realm of the Spirit and in truth.

(John 4:23-24 TPT)

God is committed to teaching us how to see, so the Holy Spirit is our tutor. Those who worship in Spirit and truth learn to follow the Holy Spirit's lead. The throne of God is established on the praises of His people (see Psalm 22:3) and is the center of His Kingdom.

Holy Spirit, teach me about the nature of Your Kingdom...

_____

_____

_____

_____

I pledge my life to worshiping God who deserves all my praise...

_____

_____

_____

_____

EVENING

The Value of His Presence

Yet a time is coming and has now come when the true
worshipers will worship the Father in the Spirit and in truth,
for they are the kind of worshipers the Father seeks....

(John 4:23-24 NIV)

In the worship environment we learn things that go way beyond what our intellect can grasp (see Ephesians 3:20). The greatest lesson is realizing the value of His Presence. Psalmist David saw into God's realm, writing, *"I have set the Lord continually before me; because He is at my right hand, I will not be shaken"* (Psalm 16:8 AMP). He saw God daily with eyes of faith—a priceless revelation given by God to true worshipers.

I will worship my Father in Spirit and truth...

_____

_____

_____

_____

I will open my heart to worship Him...

_____

_____

_____

_____

Day 87

God's Anointing

Anoint them just as you anointed their father, so they may serve me
as priests. Their anointing will be to a priesthood that
will continue throughout their generations.

(Exodus 40:15 NIV)

Jesus needed the Holy Spirit to fulfill His mission to finish the Father's work (see John 4:34). Likewise, we must be clothed with the Holy Spirit for supernatural ministry. God's anointing brings supernatural results, allowing Jesus to do only what He saw His Father do, and say only what He heard His Father say. The Holy Spirit revealed the Father to Jesus—He will do so for us.

Jesus needed You, Holy Spirit, so I too need to be filled with the anointing of the Father...

_____

_____

_____

_____

I can't do it without You, Holy Spirit, come...

_____

_____

_____

_____

Day 87

The Anointing and the Holy Spirit

Anoint them as you did their father, so they may also serve me as priests. With their anointing, Aaron's descendants are set apart for the priesthood forever, from generation to generation.

(Exodus 40:15 NLT)

The spirits of hell are at war against the anointing; without the anointing, humankind is no threat to their dominion. Jesus' concern for humanity was applauded, His humility was revered, His anointing released the supernatural—that is what the religious leaders of His day rejected. The supernatural invasion of God Himself in the Person of the Holy Spirit equips people for supernatural endeavors.

When I depend on God and His Spirit, He is delighted and I am...

_____

_____

_____

_____

I admit I'm needy—and I thankfully acknowledge God meets my needs when...

_____

_____

_____

_____

Teaching and Doing

This man came to Jesus by night and said to Him, "Rabbi, we know
that You are a teacher come from God; for no one can do
these signs that You do unless God is with him."

(John 3:2 NKJV)

Jesus never separated teaching from doing. God-type teachers don't just talk—they do. Jesus' ultimate example in ministry was combining the proclamation of the Gospel with signs and wonders. He commanded His disciples, *"And as you go, preach, saying, 'The kingdom of heaven is at hand.' Heal the sick, cleanse the lepers, raise the dead, cast out demons. Freely you have received, freely give"* (Matthew 10:7-8 NKJV).

Father, forgive me for all the ways that I haven't practiced what I preach...

_____

_____

_____

_____

Father, help me to seize opportunities to...

_____

_____

_____

_____

EVENING

In the Trenches

After dark one evening, he came to speak with Jesus. "Rabbi," he said, "we all know that God has sent you to teach us. Your miraculous signs are evidence that God is with you."

(John 3:2 NLT)

As believers of God who teach, we must do so with power and signs and wonders. Bible teachers who restrict themselves to mere words limit their gift and may unintentionally lead believers to pride by increasing knowledge without an increased awareness of God's Presence and power. In the trenches of Christlike ministry is where we learn to become totally dependent on God.

It's so much easier to leave God's anointing in the comfortable realm of the theoretical, but...

_____

_____

_____

_____

God's love is tangible, shown in how He...

_____

_____

_____

_____

In That Day

It shall come to pass in that day that his burden will be taken away from your shoulder, and his yoke from your neck, and the yoke will be destroyed because of the anointing oil.

(Isaiah 10:27 NKJV)

The Presence of God is realized in the anointing—God covering us with His power-filled Presence. The supernatural happens when we walk in the anointing! For the most part, the anointing has been hoarded by the Church for the Church. But in the Kingdom of God, we only get to keep what we give away. His wonderful Presence is to be taken to the world.

I know God placed me strategically in the world to release His Kingdom...

_____

_____

_____

_____

God, help me connect with the people who are on Your heart...

_____

_____

_____

_____

Because of the Anointing

It shall come to pass in that day that his burden will be taken away
from your shoulder, and his yoke from your neck, and the
yoke will be destroyed because of the anointing oil.

(Isaiah 10:27 NKJV)

We owe the world a Spirit-filled life, an encounter with God. Without the fullness of the Holy Spirit in and on us, we don't give God surrendered vessels to flow through. Salvation was the immediate goal, but the ultimate goal on earth was the fullness of the Spirit in believers. Getting us to Heaven isn't as challenging as getting Heaven into us!

Only here on earth do I get to partner with God to bridge the gap...

_____

_____

_____

_____

Partnering with God means releasing healing, restoration of a broken world, and...

_____

_____

_____

_____

Presence-Focused

*No, O people, the Lord has told you what is good, and this is
what he requires of you: to do what is right, to love mercy,
and to walk humbly with your God.*

(Micah 6:8 NLT)

Heaven's culture is first and foremost Presence-focused. Everything in Heaven is connected to and thrives because of the Presence of God. There is nothing in Heaven that exists apart from His Presence. He is the beauty of that world. As worshipers, we are exposed to the surpassing greatness of His world. As a result, we are called to implement His values here.

Being Presence-focused starts today in my heart, home, workplace, and...

_____

_____

_____

_____

I can affect the culture of peace so that it looks more like the culture of Heaven by...

_____

_____

_____

_____

Day 90

What the Lord Requires

He has shown you, O mortal, what is good. And what does
the Lord require of you? To act justly and to love mercy
and to walk humbly with your God.
(Micah 6:8 NIV)

Under God's lordship in Heaven, everyone is celebrated for who they are, without anyone stumbling over who they're not. Every feature of every life is beautiful and valuable. The measure of Heaven to earth is seen in the importance we place on His Presence, His values, and His lifestyle. When His world impacts our daily lives, Heaven's culture becomes real and measurable, now.

The Bible says God wants to be involved in every aspect of my life, including...

_____

_____

_____

Each outpouring of God's Spirit shifts the atmosphere more and more toward Heaven, which means...

_____

_____

_____

Day 91

The Priority of Wisdom

Wisdom is so priceless that it exceeds the value of any jewel.
Nothing you could wish for can equal her.
(Proverbs 8:11 TPT)

Pursuing wisdom is prioritized much like to *"seek first the Kingdom of God"* is in the New Testament. Throughout Proverbs, seeking wisdom releases the blessing of God in all areas of life. Whether health, finances, position and title, or the beauty of meaningful relationships, all are enhanced and enabled through our prioritized pursuit of wisdom. This journey brings us to the wonderful discovery that wisdom is also a person. Jesus is our wisdom (see 1 Corinthians 1:30).

Jesus, You are the Person of wisdom living inside me to...

_____

_____

_____

_____

Jesus, help me to tap into Your Presence and the wisdom found there...

_____

_____

_____

_____

Day 91

No Comparison

*For wisdom is better than rubies, and all the
things one may desire cannot be compared with her.*
(Proverbs 8:22 NKJV)

Wisdom is a Person, so living in wisdom is a relationship where we learn to truly see through His eyes, gaining His perspective. And it is that perspective that enables faith. It could be said that wisdom gives faith a context in which to function. In the same way that the banks of a river give direction to the water, so wisdom gives faith a direction toward a godly target.

God created me to dream big so I'd need to rely on His wisdom, Presence, and perspective to see my dreams...

_____

_____

_____

_____

He is waiting to pour out His Presence so I can reflect His glory when I...

_____

_____

_____

_____

Exercised Senses

But solid food belongs to those who are of full age, that is,
those who by reason of use have their senses
exercised to discern both good and evil.

(Hebrews 5:14 NKJV)

Most every believer knows that the Holy Spirit lives within and that He will never leave. That knowledge is a vital biblical truth—but truth is to be known by experience. Knowing He is my Provider is reassuring—but does little good if I don't seek Him for provision. The concept of salvation does me no good unless I'm saved. The abiding Presence of the Holy Spirit must become a felt reality.

Sometimes I'm scared to share the desires of my heart...

_____

_____

_____

_____

I repent from hiding and will reveal every area of need to You, Lord...

_____

_____

_____

_____

Recognizing Right and Wrong

Solid food is for those who are mature, who through training have the skill to recognize the difference between right and wrong.

(Hebrews 5:14 NLT)

Everything about us—minds, emotions, physical bodies—is designed to recognize and dwell in the manifest Presence of God. The Holy Spirit abiding with us must always affect how we do life—life lived with a consciousness of Him affecting our faith, attitudes, conduct, everything. We often speak of using faith for a miracle, which is right and good. What if we used our faith to discover God with us?

The Lord of my life is real, not in theory only. He is...

_____

_____

_____

_____

I lay my life at God's feet, placing my dreams in His hands, trusting Him to...

_____

_____

_____

_____

Religious Bias and Arrogance

*Jesus reached out his hand and touched the leper and said,
"Of course I want to heal you—be healed!" And instantly,
all signs of leprosy disappeared!*

(Matthew 8:3 TPT)

Having respect for the world before their conversion is an unusually important value. That is not to say that we condone ungodliness, carnality, or any
such thing. It's just wise to recognize the hand of God at work in environments where we have little or no influence. Religious bias and arrogance can
keep us from caring for people, and can become part of our mindset.

As I go about my day, Holy Spirit, show me people I can care for in specific
ways...

Give me Your perspective so I have courage to speak...

Immediately Cleansed

*Then Jesus put out His hand and touched him, saying,
"I am willing; be cleansed." Immediately his leprosy was cleansed.*
(Matthew 8:3 NKJV)

The sanctifying Presence and power of God changes the equation in our dealings with the world. It used to be that the only safe place for believers was to stay away from people living unrighteously. When you touched a leper in the Old Testament, you became unclean. But in the New Testament, when Jesus touched a leper, the leper became clean. Jesus gave us the commission to do the same. The Presence and power of God dramatically and positively effects our surroundings.

You have been chosen to host My Presence on the earth.

_____

_____

_____

_____

I trust in God's redemptive power and will release it generously...

_____

_____

_____

_____

Day 94

MORNING

Different Realms of Thinking

The sum total of all your words adds up to absolute truth,
and every one of your righteous decrees is everlasting.

(Psalm 119:160 TPT)

Christians don't always fare well in a setting of discussing controversial ideas—especially if we use Scripture to prove our point. It makes sense in our realm of thinking—but usually indicates how out of touch we are with people who don't value the Bible. Sometimes we even feel good about being rejected, which is normally the outcome. Remember, we don't get any points when we suffer as fools.

May I respond to controversial topics with God's wisdom and compassion...

_____

_____

_____

Lord, help me to translate the truth found in Your Word to a people who don't yet value You...

_____

_____

_____

Day 94

The Truth

*The entirety of Your word is truth, and every
one of Your righteous judgments endures forever.*
(Psalm 119:160 NKJV)

The Bible carries the power and Presence of God for the complete transformation of a life, city, and nation. But it's not always the best to quote
Scripture. I'm not saying God can't use it. But in that context, it's best to
speak out of biblical intelligence (applying biblical principles without
directly quoting the Bible), communicating the absolutes of Scripture without requiring belief in the Bible. The law of God is written in the heart and
awakens God-given conviction to truth.

I will reach out to people in any way God leads...

I will not be scared to speak their language to bridge the gap between...

MORNING

No-Limit Affection

There is no limit to our affection for you,
but you are limited in your own affection [for us].
(2 Corinthians 6:12 AMP)

Experiencing the glory of God thrills me more than anything. The glory is the manifest Presence of Jesus and the Source of life itself. To live in His unlimited glory means exploring the great delight of who God is. Our daily exponential exploration continues throughout eternity because God is unlimited. We don't wait for Heaven—it starts now. Directing our affections toward Him literally draws us into encounters with the person of Christ.

Holy Spirit, remind me throughout my day today to turn my affection to God...

_____

_____

_____

_____

I will train my affections to remain on Him, so every moment is encountering Him in ways that...

_____

_____

_____

_____

Day 95

Anchored Affection

We are not withholding our affection from you,
but you are withholding yours from us.
(2 Corinthians 6:12 NIV)

If I'm withholding my affection or if my affection is heading in wrong directions or I'm entangled in worry, I'm robbed of a delightful journey with Christ. But when my affections are truly anchored into Him, the Presence of God manifests in simple and profound ways. My thoughts, values, and perception of circumstances are recalibrated. In the glory, everything is changed by my time in His Presence.

Anchoring myself in God brings me peace, stability, and joy no matter what storm is...

_____

_____

_____

_____

I will rest in the shelter of God's Presence through the focus of my affection...

_____

_____

_____

_____

A Presence-Based, Worshiping Culture

Yet I know that you are most holy; it's indisputable.
You are God-Enthroned, surrounded with songs, living
among the shouts of praise of your princely people.

(Psalm 22:3 TPT)

We need to focus on giving Him glory—with worship as the goal. Whatever the manifestation, we are to be overwhelmed by the One who is so kind and good. Scripture says that God inhabits the praises of His people; so to be a Presence-based culture, we have to be a worshiping culture. Worship for His glory must be the top priority.

Your kindness in my life will be at the forefront of my mind today, God...

_____

_____

_____

_____

I worship and praise You with all that I have and am, because of who You are!

_____

_____

_____

_____

The Holy One

Yet you are enthroned as the Holy One; you are the one Israel praises.
(Psalm 22:3 NIV)

We don't worship to get things from the Holy One; we worship because of His worth. We worship because we acknowledge who He is. Believers who come daily before the Lord with lifted hands and a voice of praise, ministering to Him deeply and profoundly, interact with the Presence and the glory of God through the Holy Spirit. In His Presence and glory, we are being discipled and mentored in worship and praise. God wants us to sense the moving of His Holy Spirit.

I love spending time with God as He is...

_____

_____

_____

_____

When I set my eyes on Him I allow His Presence to work...

_____

_____

_____

_____

His Redemption Army

This is why I wait upon you, expecting your
breakthrough, for your word brings me hope.
(Psalm 130:5 TPT)

Believers are to transform the world, because we are people of His Presence, people of His glory. The Lord is raising up an army who have His heart and can display His power. He is raising up an army who live with hope, knowing Jesus has a purpose and a plan for the earth. He will be successful through His people who have said yes to Him and recognize His leading.

Thank You, Lord, that I get to partner with Your plan of redemption for the world by...

_____

_____

_____

_____

You have won the victory, and I get to be part of it all when I...

_____

_____

_____

_____

EVENING

Waiting and Hoping

I wait for the Lord, my soul waits, and in His word I do hope.
(Psalm 130:5 NKJV)

There are times when the Presence of God is so strong that we must adjust everything to what He is doing in that moment. God is training us to be stewards of His Presence, to enter various environments and see the Holy Spirit bring about change. People of great faith and hope are rising up, believing that nothing is impossible. God's nature is goodness; testify of Him—knowing that His Presence makes all the difference.

The Savior of the world has already come, and I'm invited into His victory over sin and destruction...

_____

_____

_____

_____

I won't worry—I know God's plans will succeed because He knows...

_____

_____

_____

_____

From Glory to Glory

*But we all, with unveiled face, beholding as in a mirror the glory
of the Lord, are being transformed into the same image
from glory to glory, just as by the Spirit of the Lord.*

(2 Corinthians 3:18 NKJV)

True revival calls people to pursue God and pursue their purpose in history and to partner with Him in establishing His dominion over all things. The Holy Spirit doesn't come to give us a shot in the arm; He comes to help us run the race and pass the baton to the next generation so Kingdom momentum will increase with each succeeding generation.

Thank You, Lord, that I get to be part of an advancing army that will...

_____

_____

_____

_____

I will declare Your increasing authority over my life that needs Your redemptive power...

_____

_____

_____

_____

His Glorious Image

So all of us who have had that veil removed can see and reflect the glory of the Lord. And the Lord—who is the Spirit—makes us more and more like him as we are changed into his glorious image.

(2 Corinthians 3:18 NLT)

We can see history from a clear perspective and increase our experience of the transforming power our inheritance. God will train us to walk in our destiny in this hour if we embrace the challenge to study, teach, and experience it. We can enable this and the next generation to step into their identity and purpose as children of God.

God wants me to remember the legacy of faith-filled believers who...

_____

_____

_____

_____

I thank God for giving me His perspective to reveal...

_____

_____

_____

_____

Day 99

Realms of Love

When Jesus saw what was happening, he became indignant with his
disciples and said to them, "Let all the little children come to me
and never hinder them! Don't you know that God's
kingdom realm exists for such as these?"
(Mark 10:14 TPT)

Biblical faith explores the Kingdom realm with the delight and pleasure of
a well-loved child. Jesus teaches that the Kingdom of God belongs to those
who are childlike. Adults take fewer and fewer risks as they get older. But
children tirelessly explore. When our faith explores His goodness, we are
most like the children Jesus honored and celebrated.

I want to explore God's goodness starting now...

_____

_____

_____

_____

God, lead me into to realms of Your love. I will eagerly follow You...

_____

_____

_____

_____

EVENING

Such Is the Kingdom

But when Jesus saw it, He was greatly displeased and said to
them, "Let the little children come to Me, and do not forbid them;
for of such is the kingdom of God."
(Mark 10:14 NKJV)

Everything about God is extreme in the best possible sense. He is infinitely good, holy and powerful, infinitely beautiful, loving, and glorious. But none of the endless traits confine Him. Each virtue gives us a glimpse into what is beyond measure, but open for observation. We could take one trait and explore it for eternity, and still not come close to exhausting the depths of who He is.

I will dive deeply into His Presence to learn more about...

_____

_____

_____

_____

Like an eager child, I can approach my heavenly Father and receive...

_____

_____

_____

_____

Day 100

Absolute Freedom

So now the case is closed. There remains no accusing voice of
condemnation against those who are joined in
life-union with Jesus, the Anointed One.
(Romans 8:1 TPT)

Too often Christians live under the influence of yesterday's failures, blemishes, and mistakes. When we do, that lie halts the renewing of our minds and keeps us from living in the "everyday miraculous" that should be normal for every born-again believer. When joined with Jesus, accusing voices have no place in our minds. God's forgiveness is complete—the case is closed, the failure forgotten!

Thank You, Jesus, that I can walk in absolute freedom from...

_____

_____

_____

_____

I am pure in Your sight, Lord, help me to live that truth every day...

_____

_____

_____

_____

Not Guilty

*Therefore there is now no condemnation [no guilty verdict, no
punishment] for those who are in Christ Jesus [who believe
in Him as personal Lord and Savior].*

(Romans 8:1 AMP)

Living under yesterday's condemnation never makes us more humble. If anything, it keeps us focused on ourselves instead of on the Lord. It's much more difficult to humbly receive forgiveness we don't deserve than to walk in false humility, cloaked in yesterday's shame. When we receive free forgiveness, the One who gave it to us is honored. When He is honored, we are truly humbled.

I am now one with God, an equal participant in His holiness, righteousness, peace, joy, and...

What a blessing to know that God looks at me with absolute tenderness and affection. I am His...

About
Bill & Beni Johnson

BILL and **BENI JOHNSON** are the senior pastors of Bethel Church in Redding, California, and serve a growing number of churches that cross denominational lines. They are both bestselling authors—Bill of *When Heaven Invades Earth* and *Hosting the Presence;* and Beni of *The Happy Intercessor.* They have three children and ten grandchildren.

YOUR *Prophetic* COMMUNITY

Are you passionate about hearing God's voice, walking with Jesus, and experiencing the power of the Holy Spirit?

Destiny Image is a community of believers with a passion for equipping and encouraging you to live the prophetic, supernatural life you were created for!

We offer a fresh helping of practical articles, dynamic podcasts, and powerful videos from respected, Spirit-empowered, Christian leaders to fuel the holy fire within you.

Sign up now to get awesome content delivered to your inbox
destinyimage.com/sign-up

 Destiny Image